Those Beautiful Coastal Liners

THE CANADIAN PACIFIC'S PRINCESSES

ROBERT D. TURNER

W9-BZH-789

Dedicated with sincere appreciation to my friends
Dr. Wallace B. Chung and Leonard G. McCann
for their tireless efforts to preserve the
Maritime History of British Columbia.

And in memoriam, for Earl Marsh and Maurice Chandler
who loved the Princesses
and the elegance they brought to the Coast.

Without their devotion, our record of the Princesses and of the Pacific Coast would be very much poorer.

Copyright © 2001 by Robert D. Turner

ALL RIGHTS RESERVED. No part of this publication may be reproduced or used in any form or by any means, without the prior written permission of Sono Nis Press, or in case of photocopying or other reprographic copying, a licence from CANCOPY (Canadian Copyright Licensing Agency), 1 Yonge Street, Ste 1900, Toronto, Ontario, M5W 1E5

National Library of Canada Cataloguing in Publication Data

Turner, Robert D., 1947-
    Those beautiful coastal liners

    Includes bibliographical references and index.
    ISBN 1-55039-109-7

    1. British Columbia Coast Service. 2. Coastwise shipping–British Columbia–History.
3. Coastwise shipping–Pacific Coast (U.S.)–History. 4. Steamboat lines–British Columbia–History. I. Title.
HE769.T87 2001   387.5'24'09711   C2001-910020-5

Sono Nis Press gratefully acknowledges the support of the Canada Council for the Arts and the Province of British Columbia, through the British Columbia Arts Council.

Designed by Robert Turner

Page 1: The lovely *Princess Marguerite* steaming to Victoria from Seattle in the 1960s, with Trial Island in the background.
–Nicholas Morant, Canadian Pacific Archives

Page 3: Vancouver Island's coastal inlets, sheltered from the open Pacific, gave passengers a respite from the weather on the "outside," as veterans called the open coast.
–B.C. Government photo, Ken Gibson collection

Published by
SONO NIS PRESS
P.O. Box 5550, Stn. B
Victoria, British Columbia V8R 6S4
Tel: (250) 598-7807
http://www.islandnet.com/sononis/
sono.nis@islandnet.com

Printed and bound in Canada

The Canada Council | Le Conseil des Arts
for the Arts | du Canada

Contents

"When the *Princess Maquinna* was approaching Ahousaht, when it was still on the other side of Catface Mountain, you could feel it. You could hear it. This was back when there were no sounds from machinery; when a man could go to the top of the hill and call people to a feast in the traditional way. You could feel it in your body; it's almost imperceptible, but you could feel it. It's gentle, but it's also shocking because it's such a contrast.... A huge machine like that, ploughing the waves, disturbs the environment, sets your heart a-pumping... because it was so quiet normally. It was very dramatic. This would only be true in the summertime, though; in the wintertime the waves would be roaring too loudly."

–Dr. Richard Atleo, Chief Umeek of Ahousaht, remembering the arrival of the *Princess Maquinna*.

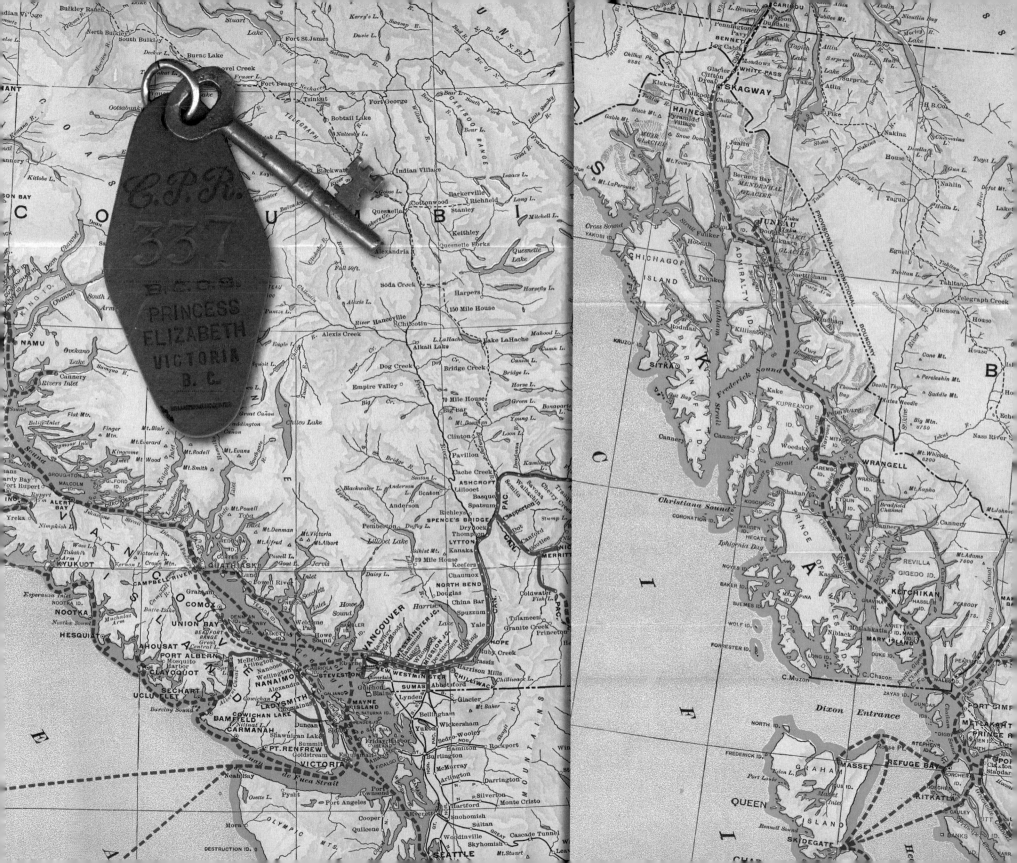

Preface & Acknowledgments

THE CANADIAN PACIFIC RAILWAY's *Princesses* on the British Columbia coast have been a passion of mine for many years. My interest goes back to some of my earliest memories travelling between Victoria and Vancouver on such lovely old steamers as the night boat sisterships *Princess Joan* and *Princess Elizabeth*. And much later I remember watching with great sadness the last voyages of the *Princess Marguerite* on the Seattle run; I couldn't watch her being towed away, leaving Victoria for the last time. I can remember only the last decades of the *Princesses* on the British Columbia, Washington and Alaskan coasts. Their story began in the early 1900s with roots going back to at least the 1880s. Their reign of peak service lasted just six decades but it was an important period along the coast and a time of great transition.

Indelible memories remain: perfectly poached salmon served on CPR china with linen table cloths in the immaculate dining room; of watching a coffee cup chatter its way across a table top in the coffee shop of the aging and sometimes vibration-prone *Princess Elaine* as she reversed direction and gathered headway; the warmth and luxury of fresh linen sheets in the bunks of the night boats; the lights of Vancouver fading away as we passed under Lions Gate Bridge not long after midnight; the deep blast of the *Princess Joan's* whistle echoing off the north shore mountains as she backed out into Burrard Inlet; hearing the news on the radio that unbelievably the *Princess Kathleen* had sunk; Trial Island off Victoria in the early morning light as rain and spray splashed on the porthole of the night boat stateroom; sitting on suitcases one holiday weekend when every seat and stateroom was taken on the *Princess Pat*; steaming out of Seattle's Elliott Bay on the *Marguerite* with the breathtaking backdrop of the Olympic Mountains; and watching a procession of *Princesses* clearing Victoria on a long ago Thanksgiving weekend when the wind and rain blew in from the Pacific, sweeping over the decks as we built up speed heading for Vancouver.

This book is a sharing of some of those memories mingled with the experiences of other travellers and crew members in an affectionate album of photographs of the beautiful *Princesses*. Although this book is not a detailed historical study, it draws on many primary sources and presents new material and photographs I have accumulated since the publication of *The Pacific Princesses* in 1977. I have emphasized several of the *Princesses* to tell the story of the fleet partly because they are personal favourites–the *Princess Victoria*, the *Kathleen*, the *Maquinna*, the *Joan* and *Elizabeth* and the second *Marguerite*–and because they were such important vessels in the unfolding story of the Coast Service. I have also made only passing mention to the Canadian National's *Princes* because they will be the subject of another book.

Many people have helped me over the years with photos, information, recollections, encouragement and shared enthusiasm for these beautiful, stately and elegant coastal steamships and here I can mention only a few. Special thanks are due to Maurice Chandler, Dr. Wally Chung, Leonard McCann and Earl March and to many other friends: Commodore Lester G. Arellanes, Dr. Richard Atleo (Chief Umeek), Art Bain, Capt. L. C. Barry, M.B.E., Jeri Bass, Clinton Betz, Milton Braley, Richard Brown, Harry Burchill, Lance Camp, Lorne Campbell, Philip Chandler, Elsie Claxton, Rick Coleman, Chief Earl Maquinna George, Ken Gibson, Norman Gidney, Tom Goodlake, Averill Harp, Austin D. Hemion, Patrick O. Hind, P. A. Hole, Don and Phyllis Horne, Merv Hughes, John Illman, Edie James, Capt. L. Hamilton Johnston, O.B.E., Ken Knox, John Kung, Edna Lake, Dr. W. Kaye Lamb, Jack Lenfesty, Ruth Lomas, Bryan McGill, Ross McLeod, Dr. Ken Mackenzie, Jack Meredith, Glen Stewart Morley, Dick Moyer, George Musk, John Newman, Dave Parker, Robert W. Parkinson, Albert Paull, Roger M. Perry, J. Gary Richardson, Celia Richardson, Peter Sawatzky, Lloyd Stadum, Jim Stephen, Michael Stevens, Bjarne Tokerud, Hugh Tumilty, Harry Tyson, Fred Wanstall, Gerry Wellburn, Diane Wells, Elwood White, Joe D. Williamson and Warren Wing. Sadly, many of these friends have passed away; this book is a tribute to their knowledge and love of the coast.

I am also deeply indebted to the British Columbia Archives, Victoria; the British Columbia Legislative Library, Victoria; Canadian Pacific Archives, Montreal; Canadian Pacific Railway, Vancouver; Dedman's Photo Shop, Skagway; the Maritime Museum of British Columbia, Victoria; the National Archives of Canada, Ottawa; the Provincial Archives of Alberta, Edmonton; the Puget Sound Maritime Historical Society, Seattle; the Royal British Columbia Museum (sometimes credited as RBCM), Victoria; the Vancouver

Maritime Museum; Special Collections, the Vancouver Public Library; and the Yukon Archives, Whitehorse, for the use of their invaluable collections of documents and photographs.

For their important suggestions and comments on the manuscript and help in many ways, my sincere thanks go to Peter Corley-Smith, Milton Braley, Patrick O. Hind, Martin Lynch, Leonard G. McCann and Dr. Wally Chung. Special thanks to my wife Nancy for editorial suggestions, to Sarah, Molly and Kate for their companionship and assistance with photography and to my mother Isabella for her encouragement and recollections of the *Princesses*. Every author needs a publisher and I have been fortunate to have an excellent one who is also a good friend: Diane Morriss of Sono Nis Press. Diane and Heather Keenan of Sono Nis Press and Jim Brennan have made the production of this book a pleasure. Jim contributed his experience and graceful touch to the preparation of the book and to the scanning and restoration of the photos.

Finally a word about ships and names. The *Princesses*, although certainly worthy of the more dignified term ship, were often called boats by the people who knew them best. Even Capt. Troup often called his finest vessels "boats" in his letters to senior Canadian Pacific officials. Of course the *Princess Joan* or the *Elizabeth* on the late night sailings were always the "night boats" or the "midnight boats." In that spirit, I have used the terms that seem most appropriate to the time and passage. Similarly, I have continued the tradition of referring to the *Princesses* as "she;" calling the *Marguerite* or the *Kathleen* "it" is not fitting or sufficiently respectful.

The beautiful *Princess Marguerite* on the famous Triangle Route on a summer day in the late 1930s. –Nicholas Morant, Canadian Pacific Archives

Arrival of C.P.R. Steamer, Victoria, B.C.

7916. Canadian Pacific "Princess" Steamer, Vancouver-Victoria-Seattle Service.

ALASKA

PRINCESS LINE

PASSENGER LIST

To
3 CITIES
BY
3 FUNNELS

SEATTLE-VICTORIA-VANCOUVER

DAILY SERVICE

CANADIAN PACIFIC RAILWAY CO.

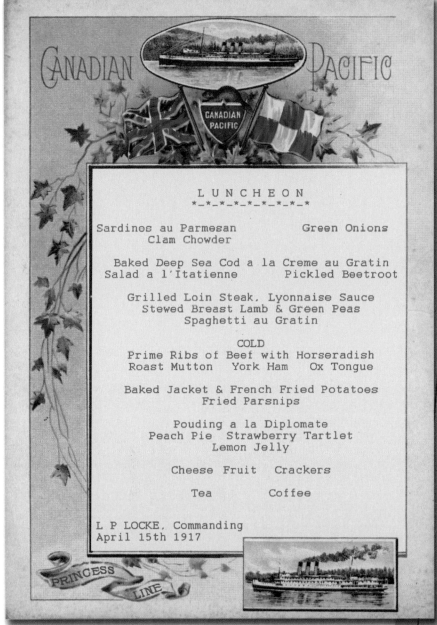

CANADIAN PACIFIC

LUNCHEON
--*-*-*-*-*-*-*

Sardinos au Parmesan   Green Onions
Clam Chowder

Baked Deep Sea Cod a la Creme au Gratin
Salad a l'Itatienne   Pickled Beetroot

Grilled Loin Steak, Lyonnaise Sauce
Stewed Breast Lamb & Green Peas
Spaghetti au Gratin

COLD
Prime Ribs of Beef with Horseradish
Roast Mutton   York Ham   Ox Tongue

Baked Jacket & French Fried Potatoes
Fried Parsnips

Pouding a la Diplomate
Peach Pie   Strawberry Tartlet
Lemon Jelly

Cheese   Fruit   Crackers

Tea   Coffee

L P LOCKE, Commanding
April 15th 1917

PRINCESS LINE

Early Canadian Pacific advertising brochures, timetables and postcards portrayed the steamers along the British Columbia and Alaskan coasts. On this page is a steward's badge and two menus from the *Princess Line*, above, from April 15, 1917 featuring in the decorations the *Princess Charlotte* and the *Princess Victoria*. At right is the *Princess Victoria's* Christmas menu from 1916 which included Esquimalt Oysters on the half shell, roast turkey, and Christmas plum pudding with hard and cognac sauces. —Facing page, Author's collection. This page, Dr. W. B. Chung collection above; Badge, Earl March collection, Royal BC Museum; and RBCM at right

"Well, he was an ingenious man that first found out eating and drinking"
—Swift

MENU

"He was a bold man that first ate an Oyster"—Swift
Esquimalt Oysters on Half Shell
Queen Olives   Salted Almonds

"Bring no further enemy to you than the constraint of hospitable zeal"
Creme de Volaille   Crout au Pot

"Take every creature in of every kind"—Pope
Boiled White Fish, Sauce Maitre d'Hotel

"Bestrewed with Lettuce and cool Salad Herbs"
Celery en Branche   Stuffed Beets

"Give us the luxuries of life and we will dispense with its necessaries"
—Motley
Grilled Lambs' Sweetbreads
Baked Cumberland Ham au Champagne
Pineapple Fritters, Sherry Wine Sauce

"Things which in hungry mortals' eyes find favor"—Byron
Roast Turkey, Chestnut Dressing and Cranberry Sauce
Roast Sirloin of Beef with Yorkshire Pudding

"Socrates brought Philosophy from the clouds, but the Englishmen dragged her into the kitchen"—Hegel
Creamed Artichokes   Brussels Sprouts
Boiled and Brown Potatoes

"Fat Olives and Pistachio's fragrant nut, and the pine's tasteful apple"
Christmas Plum Pudding, Hard and Cognac Sauces
Mince Pies   Wine Jelly, Chantilly   Peach Cardinal
Glace a la Vanille, Gaufrettes   Christmas Cake
Fruits Varies   Nuts and Raisins

"Hail! wedded nourishment"
Scotch Woodcock

"Art thou come? why my cheese, my digestion"
Fromage

"Towards eve there was Tea (a luxury to Matilda) and Ice, Fruit and Coffee"—Meridiths "Lucille"
Demi Tasse

S S. PRINCESS VICTORIA
P. J. HICKEY, COMMANDER
CHRISTMAS, 1916

Early Days of the Coast Service; The Legacy of the Princess Victoria

❧

"All property operated by C.P.R. On and After this date, May 15, 1903."

–Capt. James Troup's Manager's Log book, Victoria, B.C.

"The Princess Victoria is the fastest vessel on the Pacific, in fact, we believe the fastest vessel of her type in service on this continent..."

–Pacific Marine Review, Seattle, September 1905.

"Troup, you have a fine boat and a fast one, but I am sorry to say in my opinion, she is a white elephant."

–CPR President Sir Thomas Shaughnessy to Capt. James Troup, ca. 1903, referring to the Princess Victoria.[1]

"Everyone was delighted with the Beatrice's speed and luxury. She was a gentleman's club afloat with a special lounge for ladies [to] get away from male stares and smoke."

–Victoria Daily Colonist. September, 1903.

The Princess Victoria passes Prospect Point, entering Vancouver Harbour about 1910. –Vancouver Public Library, 2883

CHAPTER I

A Coast Service Tradition Begins

A MARITIME LEGEND WAS BORN on the rugged Pacific Coast in 1901. The finest fleet of coastal liners ever to grace the Pacific was to grow and flourish in those long ago and simpler times. From a makeshift service known for its motley collection of old coastal steamers, freighters and antiquated paddlewheelers, the Canadian Pacific built a new and dynamic fleet of coastal steamships, renowned for speed, elegance and fine service, that became the dominant shipping presence along the coast of British Columbia, Puget Sound and southern Alaska.

The CPR named its early trans-Pacific liners the *Empress of India*, *Empress of Japan* and *Empress of China* and in a complementary scheme, all of these new coastal liners were given names that began with *Princess*. They left a regal legacy of accomplishment and quality service that was the envy of their competitors and established the standard of their times. Their story encompasses the Coast from the rain- and wind-swept "graveyard of the Pacific" on Vancouver Island to the fiords of northern British Columbia and southern Alaska. They raced down Puget Sound with excursion crowds, and they cruised through the Gulf Islands on warm summer evenings to the strains of a dance band when the water was so calm and dark it looked like waxed ebony. They groped through days and nights of fog in passages hardly charted, they beat through storms that lesser vessels and crews would have feared to challenge, and they carried honeymooners and loggers, fish cannery workers and tourists, soldiers and school children, families and lovers. And in just 60 years nearly all of these beautiful steamships were gone. Before long only the *Princess Marguerite* remained, but for an all too brief time. Soon even this grand old steamship was gone, leaving only memories. This is their story and some of those memories.

By the end of the 19th Century, pressure was mounting all along the British Columbia coast for improved steamship services, particularly between Vancouver and Victoria. "The Canadian Pacific Navigation Company," lamented the *Daily Colonist* on August 12, 1899, "is a dull, foggy and antiquated institution. They are out of joint in this age of activity: barnacles on the wheel of progress, and high time they were bonused to the boneyard, to there sleep forever. Are they to continue for all time sacrificing this northern country for the sake of keeping two or three old tubs—one boat that up to this very day uses candles in the staterooms—afloat and trying to do business with lines that have electricity in their make-up."

The Canadian Pacific Navigation Company (CPN), formed in 1883 from the Hudson's Bay Company fleet and the Pioneer Line owned by Capt. John Irving and other partners, was woefully short of new tonnage. Its last major vessel, the *Islander*, was built in 1888 and was a fine steamer but the service was increasingly inadequate for the growing traffic. The Canadian Pacific Railway was well aware of these shortcomings and also that the situation was costing it customers and impeding the commercial development of the coast.

In January 1901, the CPR acquired the CPN company's stock and operations for an investment of $531,000.[2] After the retirement of the CPN's mortgages, the fleet was formally transferred to the Canadian Pacific in March, 1903, and in May the steamship service officially became the British Columbia Coast Service of the CPR which in later years was called the British Columbia Coast Steamship Service.[3] Meanwhile, the CPR began the long and costly process of replacing the obsolete vessels and developing the coastal shipping services. For the CPR, its new maritime venture was equivalent to the construction of a system of railway branch lines extending to the most important communities and industries along the coast from its terminus in Vancouver.

One of the CPR's first and most important moves was to appoint Capt. James W. Troup superintendent of the service.[4] When Troup moved to Victoria from Nelson, B.C. to take over the management of the new coastal steamship service, he was 46, trim and handsome with a full mustache and showing a confidence in his smile that came of long experience with ships and the conditions on the Pacific Coast. His reputation as a riverboat captain, as a capable and efficient manager, as well as a talented designer of steamships, was formidable. Troup had been the manager of the Columbia & Kootenay Steam Navigation Company, which operated a fleet of sternwheelers in the Kootenay district of southeastern British Columbia. Over the winter of 1896-97 this fleet was taken over by the Canadian Pacific to become the railway's British Columbia Lake & River Service and Troup continued as manager. He oversaw the modernization and expansion of the fleet as well as the construction of a dozen sternwheelers intended for service between Wrangall, Alaska, and Glenora, on the Stikine River, in northern British Columbia, at the time of the Klondike Gold Rush in 1897-1898. Canadian Pacific management was obviously impressed by this brash, strong and tough young-looking man who had grown up on the lower Columbia running sternwheelers out of Portland before he was old enough to shave.

What went through Troup's mind as he walked along the old planked wharf of the Hudson's Bay Company, overlooking Victoria's waterfront that first winter day in 1901? Before him were a few of the ships he would run for the largest company in the country. He knew all too well the criticisms of the fleet that had become so frequent in the papers

Victoria's Inner Harbour as James Troup would have seen it when he took over the management of the Canadian Pacific Navigation fleet in 1901. The new Parliament Buildings are in the background, the *Islander* is at left with the small Puget Sound steamer *Utopia* of the La Conner Trading & Transportation Company docked immediately behind and the Esquimalt & Nanaimo Railway's *City of Nanaimo* is approaching the dock. The CPR acquired the E&N's two steamers and their tug in 1905. —Author's Collection

Canadian Pacific Navigation Fleet Purchased by the Canadian Pacific Railway in 1901.

Vessel	Dimensions (feet)	Built	Disposal
Major Passenger Steamers (Intercity and North Coast Services)			
Charmer	200x42x13	1887	Scrapped 1935
Islander	240x42x14	1888	Sunk 1901
Sidewheelers (Intercity and North Coast Services)			
Yosemite	282x35x13	1862	Sold 1906
Princess Louise	180x30x13	1869	Sold 1906
Sternwheelers (Intercity and Fraser River Services)			
R. P. Rithet	117x33x8	1882	Sold 1909
Transfer	122x24x5	1893	Sold 1909
Beaver	140x28x5	1898	Sold 1919
Freight and Passenger Steamers (General Coastal Trade)			
Danube	216x28x21	1869	Sold 1905
Maude	113x21x9	1872	Sold 1903
Amur	216x28x11	1890	Sold 1911
Willapa	136x22x10	1891	Sold 1902
Tees	165x26x11	1893	Sold 1923
Queen City	116x27x10	1894	Scrapped 1916
Otter	128x24x11	1900	Sold 1931

Victoria's Inner Harbour in the late 1890s and early 1900s presented a busy scene. Much of the Canadian Pacific Navigation Company's fleet is in port, docked along Wharf Street. The vessels include the *Queen City*, sidewheeler *Princess Louise*, coastal liner *Islander,* small steamer *Otter* and the old Sacramento River sidewheeler *Yosemite*. Soon after the purchase of the CPN, the Canadian Pacific established new docks and terminal facilities on the south side of Victoria's harbour near the Parliament Buildings. —EARL J. MARSH COLLECTION

The iron and steel-hulled steamer *Charmer*, built in San Francisco by the Union Iron Works in 1887, proved to be a versatile and long-lived member of the fleet. In service until the mid-1930s, she spent most of her life operating between Vancouver and either Victoria or Nanaimo. Built for the Canadian Pacific Navigation Company as the *Premier* for service to Puget Sound ports, she was heavily damaged after colliding with the collier *Willamette* on October 18, 1892. Brought back to Victoria she was repaired, renamed and returned to service but, apparently to avoid lawsuits, never returned to US waters. —CYRIL LITTLEBURY, AUTHOR'S COLLECTION

In his Victoria office, Capt. Troup kept a daily Manager's Log for the fleet. On May 15, 1903, he finished his entry, which included a list of all the ships and where they were that day, with the line shown at right: "Fleet put under C.P.R. flag today." Troup's log is in the Dr. W. B. Chung collection.

Fleet put under C.P.R. flag today

Canadian Pacific Coastal Services, October, 1901
- Victoria and Vancouver, one return trip daily;
- Victoria and New Westminster, three return trips weekly;
- New Westminster to Ladner and Steveston on the Lower Fraser, one return trip daily;
- New Westminster and Chilliwack, three return trips weekly;
- Victoria and the West Coast of Vancouver Island, one trip a week with one sailing each month going as far north as Cape Scott;
- Vancouver and the Northern British Columbia Coast, once each week; and,
- Vancouver and Southeastern Alaska, at least every two weeks.[5]

Esquimalt & Nanaimo Railway Steamships Acquired by the Canadian Pacific in 1905

Vessel	Dimensions (Feet)	Built (Purchased)	Disposal
City of Nanaimo	159 x 32 x 9	1891 (1897)	Sold 1912
Joan	177 x 30 x 11	1892	Sold 1914
Czar (tug)	101 x 22 x 11	1897 (1902)	Sold 1914

The E&N steamships provided a service between Vancouver and Nanaimo and from Victoria to Nanaimo, Comox and other communities on the east coast of Vancouver Island in connection with the E&N Railway. A tug and railcar barge service between Ladysmith and Vancouver began in 1901. The E&N vessels were part of the Canadian Pacific's acquisition of the railway on Vancouver Island and expanded Coast Service routes around the Strait of Georgia.

The *Hating* was the first vessel purchased by Capt. Troup to augment the newly acquired fleet of coastal steamers. Soon renamed the *Princess May*, the trim vessel was used on the Alaska service and was a frequent visitor to Skagway where passengers could connect with the White Pass & Yukon Route's railway to Whitehorse. J. E. Lee took these unusual onboard pictures on August 21, 1902. Unfortunately, the people are not identified, but the distinguished gentleman may be Capt. James Troup. –Barley Collection, 5164, Yukon Archives; Brown collection, B2111, B2118, Provincial Archives of Alberta

and in shipping circles. As he walked along the waterfront, his greatcoat pulled around his shoulders and his bowler pulled down tightly in the wind, looking over the big sidewheeler *Yosemite* that he had once captained, the old *Princess Louise* or perhaps the *Willapa* and the *Charmer*, he knew he faced a challenge that would occupy him for years to come. Of the fleet–his fleet now–most were obsolete, some so old they were overdue for scrapping, and just two or three were worth keeping for any length of time. It was clear that Troup didn't waste much time worrying because within days he was working on the designs for the new vessels that would form the basis of the fleet of the finest coastal liners yet seen on the Pacific Coast. Troup's direction was set and he would not deviate from his determination for nearly 30 years.

A farsighted and self-confident man, Troup won the support of Canadian Pacific management in developing the Coast Service. He needed to expand and develop routes that would reflect and direct the demands for steamship services for several decades to come. But to begin, he had to work with the services and the vessels he inherited. Using the talents he developed on the Columbia River and during his earlier years around Puget Sound, he refined plans for new steamships that would exceed in speed and service standards anything a competitor might bring to the Coast. His coastal liners would complement the best accommodations the railway offered its patrons on its trains and in its fine hotels.

Just two large passenger steamships, the *Islander* and the *Charmer*, dating from the 1880s, could still be considered effective intercity vessels. The *Charmer* was often taxed by the high levels of traffic and her slow speed was a continuing handicap on the Victoria-Vancouver service. The *Islander*, without doubt the finest vessel in the fleet, often ran to Skagway, Alaska, traffic still being brisk following the peak of the Klondike Gold Rush, so recently the most exciting adventure story gripping the world. Troup's challenge was formidable and he took it on without hesitation. To supplement the *Islander*, early in 1901, he purchased the steamer *Hating* of 1888 vintage, a well-built, twin-screw vessel, that was later renamed the *Princess May*. Although not ideally suited to the coastal operations because of its accommodations and the single-bottom construction of its hull, it was a useful addition to the fleet that could be put in service with little delay. However, no sooner it seemed had the CPR taken control of the Canadian Pacific Navigation Company than the *Islander* was lost with 42 lives on August 15, 1901, off Douglas Island south of Juneau, Alaska. It was a stunning setback for Troup and the new Coast Service.

The Princess Victoria; The standard set

THE LOSS OF THE *Islander* made the shortage of modern tonnage even more acute and Troup rushed work on the new vessels. The first was to be the landmark *Princess Victoria*, perhaps the finest coastal liner of her era and the vessel that helped define the image and reputation of the Canadian Pacific's B.C. Coast Steamship Service for decades to come. The *Princess Victoria* was ordered in 1902 from the C. S. Swan & Hunter yards at Newcastle-on-Tyne in England. She was launched that December and sailed from England, with only minimal cabin work being finished, on January 30, 1903. Fifty-eight days later, having sailed via the Strait of Magellan at the southern tip of South America, she arrived in Victoria and proceeded on to Vancouver where her cabins and other finishing work were to be undertaken. But with the busy summer season approaching, the *Princess Victoria* was placed in service before all of the woodwork and decoration was finished.

There was something very special about the *Princess Victoria* and her engines. The *Vic*, perhaps more than any other steamship in the CPR's Coast Steamship Service, excepting perhaps the *Princess Kathleen* and *Princess Marguerite* of 1925, came as close to perfection as anyone could hope for in a steamship. Her design was elegant, the accommodations spacious and luxurious for their times and her machinery worked with a smoothness and reliability that would make marine engineers envious decades later. The *Vic* was powered by two, four-cylinder, triple-expansion engines and had ample capacity in her six single-ended Scotch marine boilers to steam at high speed without letup on what was to become the famous Triangle Route between Victoria, Seattle and Vancouver. Hawthorn, Leslie & Co. supplied the *Vic*'s engines, and legend has it they were originally destined for a warship. In any event, they were part of the original contract specifications, and apparently were based on designs used by Hawthorn, Leslie in the construction of a warship for Sweden. Their reputation for reliability and power was more than justified over their nearly 50 years of service.[6]

With the *Princess Victoria* under construction, Troup ordered a smaller wooden-hulled passenger and freight vessel, to be christened the *Princess Beatrice*. This steamer, built at the local British Columbia Marine Railways yard in Esquimalt–often called "Bullen's" for W. Fitzherbert Bullen, the shipyard's managing director–was completed in 1903 and was well received by the public although overshadowed by the bigger, faster *Princess Victoria*.

On her trials off Victoria on August 17, 1903, the *Princess Victoria* easily worked up to 19 knots (21.9 miles or 35.2 km an hour) steaming with and against the tide. But that was only the beginning of her reputation for speed.* When she entered service on the Pacific Coast

Delivery of the Princess Victoria...

"Vessel shall be completed and ready for delivery on the Tyne to the purchasers, after satisfactory trial trip, on Nov. 15th., 1902. In default builders shall pay Company £10. per working day as liquidated damages until vessel is ready for delivery. Price £66,200."

–AGREEMENT FOR THE BUILDING OF THE SS NO. 281. C.S. SWAN & HUNTER, LIMITED AND THE CANADIAN PACIFIC RAILWAY COMPANY. (CONTRACT AND SPECIFICATIONS DATED MAY 30TH., 1902.)

Breaking the Records...
From the Princess Victoria's Log:
Seattle to Victoria, April 21, 1904

9:38 a.m.	Pier No. 2 Seattle
9:52 a.m.	Four-mile Rock
10:00 a.m.	West Point
10:19 a.m.	Jefferson Head
10:30 a.m.	Apple-tree Point
10:49 a.m.	Point No Point
10:59 a.m.	Double Bluff
11:10 a.m.	Bush Point
11:25 a.m.	Marrowstone Pt.
11:35 a.m.	Point Wilson
1:00 p.m.	Brotchie Ledge
Slow bell off	
1:02 p.m.	Outer Wharf, Victoria

The total distance from Seattle to Brotchie Ledge was 69 nautical miles and the average speed of the *Princess Victoria* was 20.2 knots (23 miles or 37 km an hour) while on the run from Point Wilson to Brotchie Ledge. Across the open waters of Juan de Fuca Strait, 30 nautical miles (34.5 miles or 55.5 km) distance, her speed was 21.1 knots (about 24 miles or nearly 39 km an hour). Moreover, her boilers were not at full pressure when she pulled clear of Seattle and probably she could have done slightly better.[7]

---

*One knot equals 6,080.2 feet , 1853.24 m or 1.853 km. A speed of one knot meant that the ship travelled one nautical mile an hour.

The beautiful *Princess Victoria* steaming off Victoria on the Triangle Route. –Canadian Pacific Archives

The *Princess Vic* was powered by two, four-cylinder, triple-expansion engines built by the Hawthorn, Leslie & Co., that gave the coastal liner a remarkable reputation for speed and reliability. —VANCOUVER MARITIME MUSEUM

"In 1904 I joined the *Princess Victoria* as 5th engineer and worked getting her ready for the proposed 'Double Run' which started in May and ran into a series of accidents that would have deterred a lot of men from going any further but not Capt. Troup. Mr. T.G. Mitchell was the first Chief Engineer.

"We started off in May leaving Victoria at 7.30 a.m. arriving Vancouver around 11.30 a.m. leaving again at 1.00 p.m.—arriving back in Victoria at 5.00 to 5.15 p.m., leaving again at 7.00 arriving Seattle at 11 p.m. and leaving Seattle at midnight arriving back in Victoria at 6.00 am. etc... We kept this up for 2 or 3 weeks when she went ashore in First Narrows at the exact spot where the south footing for the 1st Narrows bridge now stands. Returning to Esquimalt for repairs which took quite two weeks to finish. She then resumed service and in a very short time struck something between Fiddle reef and 10 Mile Point which bent the outboard shaft on the port side which made the port engine excessively stiff to turn over; however, the edict was to carry on the best we could, until the end of the season in September. This was done by running the port engine at 90 revs or about half speed and the starboard engine at all we could get, 160 revs, or over, with the governor disconnected. This put a terrible strain on the structure on the port side...however the double run was established and the second season in 1905 came off without incident and the foundation of the B. C. Coast Service was laid on the *Victoria's* performance."

–ALEX W. DOW IN LETTERS TO EARL MARSH, [8]
FEB. 7, 1965, AND FEB. 27, 1965.

"It is doubtful if any vessel on the Pacific Coast is so well subdivided with water tight compartments, with double bottom, numerous transverse bulkheads and water tight flats. The vessel has been so designed that it would be almost impossible to sink her, even though the vessel may be loaded and two compartments punctured."

–*Pacific Marine Review*, SEATTLE, SEPTEMBER 1906.

she soon broke all of the intercity records between Victoria and Vancouver and Seattle. Her reliability became legendary.

With the cabin work and finishing being done in Vancouver and Victoria, Troup was able to oversee the standards applied. "The boat will never be successful," he wrote, "if the detail is not looked after. It is the detail which will go to make up the whole affair." He faced suggestions from Montreal and local officials that the *Victoria* be finished with single-walled cabins and rather plainly decorated, but responded with considerable finesse that he had consulted with Victoria architect Francis Mawson Rattenbury, who had designed British Columbia's new Parliament buildings, and "we can get up something slightly different from the [Great Lakes steamer] *Manitoba* and have it decorated and at the same time not costly." Plans of the local shipwright, a man named Trist, to finish her quickly and without much imagination were not at all to Troup's liking. "He proposes to seal her up with common flooring, leaving the outside of the steamer without panel. This does not compare with other boats of her class in this part of the country, and I do not think the President, or yourself," he wrote to Arthur Piers, General Superintendent of Steamships in Montreal, "would care to have unfavorable comparisons drawn after she is finished. Surely it would not do to have a boat which would not compare favorably with the *Islander*. That steamer is fresh in the minds of people here, and we must have something as good as she was at least. That boat was paneled on the outside and on the inside. Her outside saloons were double..."

Troup went on to say that, "Mr. Rattenbury, suggests that we make one large panel in the top of the door, one small panel molded in the bottom with a large panel between rooms. He suggests a pilaster made of soft wood with a little bit of papier mache decoration inside of it, with a papier mache capital at the top. He says it would be as cheap as a hard wood pilaster and would look well."[9] Troup won his struggle for control of the work on the *Princess Victoria* and she was finished to the higher standard he desired. Troup was building for the future and his vision proved well founded. The *Vic* established a standard for the rest of the *Princess* fleet and more than repaid any extra investment in finishing work by the favorable publicity and increased patronage she generated.

Determined to see his vision for the Coast Service realized, Troup nonetheless had to work within the Canadian Pacific Railway's hierarchy. Sometimes management was critical, particularly in his early years, and Troup was not reticent to respond. After the *Vic* had two accidents in 1904, President Shaughnessy was critical of Coast Service operations. Troup, not one to mince words, wrote to Arthur Piers on July 26: "Did the President ever stop to think of the fact that insurance on this Coast is higher than almost any other place in the world, and that the rates are the result of many year's experience. Would we not be foolish to pay 12 & 14 % if we could go along from year to year without accidents? I did everything that my judgment dictated to safely run the *Victoria*. I can do nothing more but go on board and run her myself. I am using my very best efforts, and it is discouraging to go on in this way. My resignation is in your hands at any time, no notice is required...." Troup's offer to resign was not accepted and his authority and respect from management grew rapidly.

Troup was in constant need of new tonnage as British Columbia and Washington State experienced a time of rapid growth and population expansion in the early 1900s and the demands on the fleet grew. On January 8, 1904, the Puget Sound Navigation Company's passenger steamer *Clallam*, serving Victoria and Puget Sound points, foundered in Juan de Fuca Strait with the loss of 54 lives. Soon the CPR was pressed to take over this service with larger, safer and more reliable steamships and Troup placed the *Princess Beatrice* on the run, adding yet another service to the growing web of routes along the coast. Then in 1905 the railway company acquired the Esquimalt & Nanaimo Railway on Vancouver Island and with it the small, aging wooden steamers *Joan* and *City of Nanaimo* as well as the tug *Czar* which was used to tow coal barges and railway barges back and forth between Vancouver and Ladysmith on Vancouver Island. The shipping services soon came under Troup's expanding mandate but inevitably added to the shortage of modern vessels.

Souvenir ribbon from the *Princess Victoria's* first excursion to Tacoma on August 22, 1903. –Dr. W. B. Chung collection

The *Princess Vic* never failed to make a striking appearance. At left, she steams past Victoria's waterfront. Carl F. Timms photographed the *Vic* in a view he titled "One of our flyers," as she pulled away from the dock in Vancouver. –NATIONAL ARCHIVES OF CANADA, PA9587 AND VANCOUVER PUBLIC LIBRARY, 2953

The Beautiful Princess Victoria...

"The dining room is finished in ivory white with mahogany trimmings, the windows being plate glass. There are seats for 90 passengers. Mahogany chairs upholstered in leather are used instead of the steamship revolving chair, it being found that the average weather encountered in the coasting trade allows for this. The after end of the main deck is occupied by the galley and pantry....

"The housework on the upper deck contains at the forward end second-class smoking room, bar, office and hand baggage room, and staterooms on either side provided with baths, hot and cold water, individual steam heat and telephone. Above this is another deck, at the forward end of which is the real feature of the vessel. An observation room is fitted with large plate glass windows entirely around the forward end and sides of the room. This room is painted in white enamel and gold, is well ventilated, well carpeted and nicely furnished with wicker arm chairs. From this room on wet and cold days a passenger may view the scenery in comfort and without exposure. There are 34 staterooms on this deck and at the after end is a smoking room, similar in arrangement to the observation room at the forward end. The smoking room is finished entirely in mahogany. The dome ceiling overhead is appropriately decorated, and there are leaded skylights.

"The vessel is lighted throughout with electricity, heated with steam, all rooms are provided with electric call bells and every stateroom is well ventilated....

"The joiner work was all finished up in Vancouver and Victoria by local mechanics. The art glass work was designed and manufactured by Messrs. Bloomfield & Sons of Vancouver... Messrs. Weiler Bros., of Victoria, manufactured the furniture, while Messrs. Lenz & Leiser and Messrs. Turner, Beeton & Co., of Victoria, furnished the blankets, bed spreads, etc., ...all made to order and woven with the company's monogram."

—*Pacific Marine Review*, Seattle, September 1906.

Luncheon menu from the *Princess Victoria's* early years. The *Vic's* full service dining saloon was a highlight of the vessel's elegant interior. The wonderful series of photographs that are reproduced on the following pages give a rare insight into the passenger accommodations on one of the early *Princesses*.[10] —Dr. W. B. Chung collection; Brigden photo, Vancouver Maritime Museum

CANADIAN PACIFIC RAILWAY COMPANY

S.S. PRINCESS VICTORIA

P. J. HICKEY, COMMANDER

LUNCHEON

Sardines Parmesan	Potted Game on Toast
Boullion in Cup	Clam Chowder

Salmon Cutlets, Tartare Sauce

Sliced Tomatoes   Crab Salad, Mayonnaise   Dressed Lettuce
Melon Mangoes

HOT { Loin Steaks, Broiled Tomatoes   Stewed Kidney with Fresh Mushrooms
Spring Chicken with Curly Bacon   Spaghetti au Gratin

COLD { Sirloin of Beef with Horseradish   Veal and Ham Pie   Ox Tongue
Fowl en Aspic Jelly   Rolled Ham

Baked Potatoes   French Fried Potatoes
Corn Cob, Butter Sauce

Apple Pie   Wine Jelly with Whipped Cream   Black Currant Tartlets
Lemon Cream Pie
Lemon Ice Cream   Cold Tapioca Custard and Fruit Sauce

CANADIAN STILTON, MacLAREN'S AND ROQUEFORT CHEESE
TEA   ASSORTED FRESH FRUIT   **COFFEE**

Passengers will confer a favor by reporting unsatisfactory service in the Dining Saloon to the Chief Steward at once, and inattention or incivility on the part of any employee in the Steward's Department to the Head Office, Victoria.

The *Princess Victoria's* interior captured the attention to detail and finish that was a hallmark of Capt. Troup's vessels. At left, the main saloon aft on the promenade deck; above, passengers enjoy the ship's forward observation lounge. The ship's pianos were always popular with passengers.
–Vancouver Maritime Museum, 6205 left, 6195 above right, and Brigden photos 6211 and 6201

The Vic's Cabins...

"There are 78 cabins, excellently lighted with electricity and thoroughly ventilated. The furnishings are all of the best and tastefully arranged. The majority of the rooms contain a large double lower berth, three feet six inches [1.1 m] wide, and a single upper berth, two feet six inches [.75 m] wide. Four staterooms, i.e., two on each side, are arranged en suite, with bath and toilet between, and are fitted with large brass beds." – BCCSS, Summer 1910 Schedule.

The beautiful staircase between the promenade deck and the "shade" deck above, was a design feature Troup incorporated into other coastal liners and Lake & River Service steamers. Staterooms opened off the long passageways on both sides of the *Princess Victoria*. They were small but comfortable, designed to accommodate passengers spending a single night on board. —Brigden photos, Vancouver Maritime Museum, 6209, 6199 and 5939

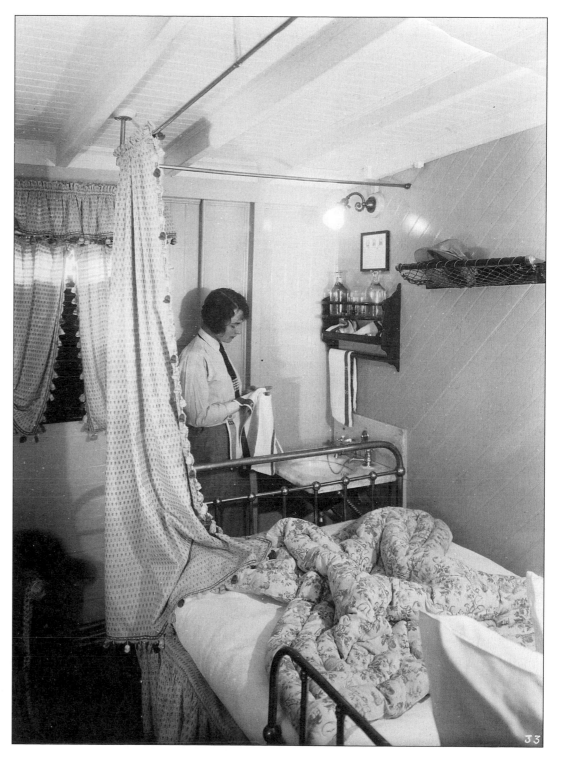

Expanding the Fleet

FOLLOWING ON THE SUCCESS OF THE *Princess Victoria*, Troup ordered another wooden steamer from the B.C. Marine Railways to augment his fleet and avoid delays in deliveries from Great Britain. This steamer, *Princess Royal*, resembling the *Princess Victoria* in her accommodations but single-stacked and slower, joined the fleet in 1907, and with the *Vic* established a new double service on an express route between Victoria, Seattle and Vancouver. Soon dubbed the "Triangle Route," it became a mainstay of the CPR service. One steamer operated in each direction around the Triangle, providing an unprecedented level of service.

Meanwhile, an even larger coastal liner was under construction at the Fairfield yards in Glasgow, Scotland. This newest vessel, the intended running mate for the *Princess Victoria*, was named the *Princess Charlotte* and she was to be one of the longest lived of all the *Princesses* although the last 16 years of her 57-year career were spent in the Mediterranean under the Greek flag. The *Charlotte* arrived in time to help Troup and his Coast Service win a protracted rate war with the Puget Sound Navigation Company over the traffic between Victoria and Seattle. With the *Charlotte* in hand, the *Royal* ran to the North Coast.

The *Charlotte* was a beautiful vessel but Troup was disappointed with her performance and fuel consumption. The problems were not fully solved until the *Charlotte* and most of the other vessels in the fleet were converted to burn oil instead of coal for their steam machinery. The *Vic* continued to hold the records for fastest runs and as the years went by she kept the *Charlotte* at bay, although their running times could be very close. By the summer of 1909, the *Charlotte* had shaved the speed on the Seattle to Victoria route between Four Mile Rock and Brotchie Ledge to 3 hours and 3 minutes but on July 7, the *Victoria* came racing back to regain the blue ribband. Her time was just 2 hours and 59 minutes. "Brotchie Ledge,"[11] reported the *Times*, "was reached at 12.19 and then the cheering began. Some of the crew nearly went wild for the record meant victory for their boat, of which they are so proud."

In just eight short years, Troup was well along towards his goal of creating the finest fleet on the Northwest Coast. In this he succeeded beyond doubt but it required the construction of several other vessels in the years leading up to the beginning of the First World War. At the same time, the Coast Steamship Service was showing a gratifying profit on its operations. In 1907, net profits of $164,510 were earned; in 1910 with an exposition in Seattle that generated heavy traffic, profits soared to $774,100, but settled back to a still respectable level of $498,958 the next year to rise to $630,714 in 1912. On an investment of $4,186,000 by 1912, the net reflected an annual return of about 15 percent.[12]

The Vic was fast...

"Fort Warden, July 20th. (Special). One of the favorite vessels used by the range-finders for practice work is the *Princess Victoria* which passes the fortifications on her runs between Seattle and Victoria twice a day. A recent recording of the steamer's speed gave her a 22-knot clip. The record has never been equalled with the register maintained by the tower man."

—*Daily Province*, VANCOUVER , JULY 20, 1907.

The *Princess Beatrice*, photographed by Cyril Littlebury at Vancouver, above, on September 21, 1926 and the *Princess May* at Victoria before her cabins were expanded. At right, the *May* in Vancouver Harbour passing a beautiful steam yacht. —AUTHOR'S COLLECTION, TWO PHOTOS; VANCOUVER PUBLIC LIBRARY, 2973

The Princess Royal...

"The queen of the Alaska steamships, was built in 1907. She was designed especially for the Alaska and Northern British Columbia Coast service. Her designers had in view safety and comfort before every other detail, and no expense was spared...

"The Dining Room, on the Main Deck, is second to none, and is one of the cheeriest spots, while the excellence of the table service [of the CPR] is well known to all travellers and will meet the approval of the most exacting."

– B.C. Coast Steamship Service, Summer 1910 Schedules.

Shown steaming through the Inside Passage to Alaska, the *Princess Royal*, at left, was a fine wooden-hulled coastal liner built in Esquimalt. Her cabin design drew from the *Princess Victoria's* but she was powered by only a single, triple-expansion engine supplied by the Bow McLachlan & Co. of Paisley, Scotland. The CPR docks, below, dominated the south side of Victoria's Inner Harbour by 1910. Three steamers are in port this sunny day, the *Princess Victoria*, the old coastal freighter *Amur* and the *Princess Beatrice*. The photo was taken from the Empress Hotel. –University of Washington Library; Royal British Columbia Museum

The Princess Charlotte...

"On either side of the central hall are twelve large special three-berth rooms, fitted up in first-class manner, with electric radiators, sofa beds, washstands, etc., and there are four rooms fitted up as bridal chambers. This unusual number has given the *Princess Charlotte* the title of 'THE HONEYMOON BOAT,'" noted a Canadian Pacific brochure from about 1910.

In 1908 the *Princess Charlotte* joined the B.C. Coast Steamship Service and ran opposite the *Princess Victoria* on the Triangle Route. Bigger than the *Vic* by over 1800 gross tons, she was 30 feet (9.1m) longer and six feet (1.8 m) wider than her running mate. Over the years her passenger license varied between 1200 and 1500 people and she featured spacious and carefully appointed accommodations.

The *Charlotte* was powered by two, four-cylinder, triple-expansion engines with cylinders 24 x 38 x 43 x 43 inches in diameter and a stroke of 33 inches. These engines served her well. Sold by the CPR in 1949 to the Typaldas Bros. of Greece, the *Charlotte* was renamed the *Mediterranean* and remained in service until 1965.

Summer Trips Around the Triangle...

"The three funnel liners are not ordinary excursion steamers, they combine sight-seeing possibilities with every known comfort for travelling. Then, too, ...special attention must be drawn to the fact that travelling over an inner route, they are at all times on smooth waters. This feature, combined with the sea air and fine scenery gives it decided advantages over other water trips."

– B.C. Coast Steamship Service, Summer 1910 Schedules.

The *Charlotte* was photographed, above right, on her arrival at Victoria after her long voyage from the Fairfield yards in Govan, Scotland. She is streaked with rust and her lounge windows and shelter deck are covered over to protect the ship from damage in heavy seas. At right, the fine steamer was captured by Cyril Littlebury leaving Vancouver. –Both Author's collection

Following pages: The Canadian Pacific's railway and steamship docks covered the south side of Burrard Inlet and were the transportation hub of British Columbia. There was a constant procession of passenger and express trains arriving or departing and the wharves were busy with coastal and ocean steamships. Steamships captured in this sweeping view include, from left, the *Princess May, Queen City,* either the *Princess Alice* or *Adelaide, Princess Victoria, Princess Royal,* one of the CPR's *Empresses* of 1891, and the CPR trans-Pacific steamer *Monteagle.* –Dr. W. B. Chung collection

C.P.R. S.S. PRINCESS CHARLOTTE VICTORIA. B.C.

The *Adelaide* was photographed in late afternoon sun in Victoria in the 1940s while the *Alice,* at right, was at the Victoria docks. —MAURICE CHANDLER ABOVE; BOTH AUTHOR'S COLLECTION

The Princess Adelaide and Princess Alice...

The nearly identical *Alice* and *Adelaide* became versatile stalwarts of the fleet for nearly 40 years. Surprisingly, they were built at different yards, the *Adelaide* by the Fairfield Shipbuilding & Engineering Company and the *Alice* by Swan, Hunter & Wigham Richardson of Newcastle. The *Adelaide* arrived in Victoria in December 1910 and the *Alice* followed on December 22, 1911 having sailed via Cape Horn. The most obvious exterior difference between the two vessels was the more extensive plating near the bow on the upper deck of the *Alice*. Over their long years with the BC Coast Steamship Service very few modifications were made to their appearance.

Their passenger capacity was 1200, although this number varied over the years, and 222 people could be accommodated in 113 staterooms. Dining room seating was 80-85. With a top speed of about 16 knots, they were intended initially for the night boat service between Victoria and Vancouver but soon were employed on many other services. These steel-hulled night boats were powered by single, four-cylinder, triple-expansion engines and in general outline resembled the *Princess Royal*. The *Adelaide*, built as a coal burner, was modified with oil burners in Seattle when repairs were carried out to her boilers but the *Alice* was fitted with oil burner equipment at her builder's yards and was the first *Princess* built to burn oil.[13]

Both steamers were sold in 1949 to the Typaldas Bros. of Piraeus, Greece, the *Alice* being renamed the *Aegaeon* and the *Adelaide* becoming the *Angelika*. The *Alice* lasted until 1966 when she was wrecked and later scrapped with the *Adelaide* being scrapped in 1967.

New steamships came in rapid succession: the *Princess Adelaide* in 1910 and the *Princess Alice* of 1911, two large, nearly identical, single-screw steamers for night boat service between Victoria, Vancouver and Seattle as well as other services; two more coastal steamers, the *Princess Mary* of 1910 and the *Princess Sophia* of 1912 for Gulf of Georgia, Alaskan and North Coast services; and the *Princess Patricia*, a fast, pioneering turbine-powered passenger vessel originally called the *Queen Alexandra*, acquired used in Great Britain in 1911 and delivered the following year, for the Vancouver to Nanaimo route. This steamer, attained a speed of 21.63 knots on her trials and originally had five propellers, two being mounted on each of the outside shafts. The steamer was damaged in a fire and Capt. Troup was originally skeptical about buying her in part because of the possible difficulties she might encounter on the long voyage to Victoria. However, he was personally reassured by Leslie Denny of Wm. Denny & Bros, whose yard built her, and the purchase, followed by a thorough reconstruction, went ahead.

Next came the *Princess Maquinna*, named at Capt. Troup's suggestion, but without cultural understanding, for the daughter of the famous Nuu-Chah-Nulth chief from what is now called Nootka Sound, who met the English navigators Capt. James Cook and later Capt. George Vancouver and Spanish Capt. Juan Francisco de la Bodega y Quadra in the late 1700s. The *Maquinna* was built at the B.C. Marine Railways' yard in 1912 and 1913, for the West Coast of Vancouver Island route. Finally, as Europe slipped closer and closer to war in 1914, two even larger intercity, turbine-powered coastal liners, the *Princess Margaret* and *Princess Irene*, were nearing completion in the Wm. Denny & Bros. yards at Dumbarton, Scotland. Costing £393,793, or about $2,000,000 by the time they were fully equipped, these were intended for the Triangle Route but they never reached the Pacific Coast; instead they became minelayers for the British Admiralty, with only the *Margaret* surviving the war. Capt. Troup travelled to Britain in 1913 to make arrangements for these fine ships which Victoria's *Daily Colonist* said, following an interview with Troup, would be "the best in the world." Two larger night boats were projected in 1912, but they were not built.[14]

All of these steamers developed a reputation of fine service but few could equal the standing of the *Princess Maquinna* whose association with the West Coast of Vancouver Island spanned over four decades. Requests for quotes were made to several well-established yards in Britain but by the time delivery costs were considered the Bullen's yard at Esquimalt was competitive. He was never disappointed in this decision because the *Maquinna* proved to be a well-built vessel, ideally suited for the rugged and demanding service that was to be her life. Launched on Christmas Eve, 1912, she was christened by Mrs. Bullen. The *Maquinna's* triple-expansion engine and two oil-fired Scotch Marine boilers that drove the little steamer at 13.5 knots (15.5 miles or 25 km an hour), came from the Bow, McLachlan yards of Paisley, Scotland, the same builder who had provided the machinery for the *Beatrice* and the *Royal* and who built the *Princess Sophia*. After her preliminary sea trials, the *Maquinna* was taken over by the CPR from the builder on July 15, 1913. Her contract price was $245,000.

With a certificate for 174 passengers when in West Coast service, her passenger accommodations provided 52 staterooms with a total of 108 berths as well as 30 berths in second class, which later were removed. Seating in the dining room was for 65 people. She was licensed to carry 500 people when in inland waters. Her normal crew was 70 and on many voyages there were more crew than passengers on the little steamer. Capt. Edward Gillam, an experienced coastal mariner, was the *Maquinna's* first master.

BROWN PHOTO

PRINCESS MARY

The Princess Mary...

Smallest of the new *Princesses*, the *Mary* was a sturdy, well-built vessel intended for Gulf of Georgia services. The little *Princess* arrived in Victoria on February 15, 1911 after a rough voyage from Scotland and following refitting, was ready to replace the small and antiquated *City of Nanaimo*. Capt. Douglas Brown took command and on her first trip on the Nanaimo-Comox-Vancouver service, with Capt. Troup and other officials on board, she was thrown open to the public for inspection. At Nanaimo, noted the *Free Press* on March 14, 1911, "they found her lavishly and luxuriously fitted up with every modern convenience, and there was general agreement that she was far and away superior to any passenger boat on the Nanaimo run [and] it is significant of the foresight of the management of the coast service in providing a vessel of such pretensions."

She was a cozy little ship, with dining room seating for 64, a central social hall on the awning deck just above, a second-class smoking room and bar forward under the pilot house, and a first-class smoking room aft on the boat deck. Staterooms had hot and cold running water, steam heat, and reading lights. Four special rooms called "bridal suites" had private shower baths for a premium price of $4.00 overnight or $3.00 for a day trip. Typical staterooms with single upper and double lower berths cost $2.50 to $3.00 (if the cabin had an additional sofa berth) although a few rooms were just $2.00 for the night or $1.00 for a day trip.

Second-class bunks were situated forward on the Lower Deck near the crew's quarters. Reflecting the priority of those pre-First World War years, she was not built to carry automobiles except for the occasional vehicle that early motorists might squeeze onto the freight deck. However, 90 head of cattle could be accommodated, because the *Mary* was built to carry everything that people needed.

Soon the *Mary's* capacity was inadequate for the traffic and the steamer was lengthened at the Yarrow's marine railway at Esquimalt. In January 1914, the *Mary* was pulled up onto the ways and cut in half. Very carefully, the stern was eased down the ways exactly 38 feet, 4 inches, and new keel sections inserted. Then the hull was built up and oil tanks were installed as part of the process of converting her to burn oil. Cabins also had to be lengthened which permitted the addition of 24 new staterooms and a new forward social hall. Second-class accommodations were increased and cargo space was enlarged by over 10,000 cubic feet (930 m³), enough for 250 tons of freight as well as more room in the lower hold. Her passenger capacity was 500 or 600 and sleeping accommodations could be provided for 160. After her reconstruction, the *Mary* was assigned to the Alaska and North Coast services but over the years she was used just about everywhere, including the West Coast of Vancouver Island and as a relief steamer and night boat on the Triangle Route. However, she was most closely associated with the Gulf Islands and Powell River routes where she worked in her autumn years during the 1930s and 40s.

The Princess Mary as built, at left, after being lengthened in 1914 above right, and easing away from the dock in Vancouver harbour in 1910. The Princess Sophia and the Puget Sound Navigation Company's Iroquois, at right, with the Princess Alice in the background at Victoria. —Brown photo and Cyril Littlebury, both author's collection; Vancouver Maritime Museum, 4218; Austin Hemion photo, Clinton Betz collection

The Princess Sophia...

Solidly built for the Alaska coastal trade, the *Princess Sophia* became a popular steamer. With a licensed capacity of 500, her 83 staterooms provided a total of 166 berths and 84 people could sleep in second class berths on the main deck. *The Daily Colonist* described her on May 21, 1912, the day after her arrival in Victoria. "Forward on the upper passageway deck is a finely built and appointed observation room, finished in maple; the dining saloon is aft on the deck below, and a spacious saloon, with staterooms handsomely furnished and appointed, at either side. The dining saloon which seats 100 [later shown as 112] is finished in mahogany with maple panels. The smoking room, set by itself in a deckhouse on the upper deck aft, is excellently and comfortably appointed—in fact the whole vessel shows that nothing has been left undone to provide for the comfort of the traveller, in keeping with CPR methods."

The *Princess Sophia*, shown at left leaving Juneau, is steaming at about 12 knots on the Alaska Service for which she was built. A typical schedule from the First World War years saw her leaving Victoria at 11:00 pm, and spending the next day in Vancouver, then stopping at her regular ports of call: Alert Bay, Prince Rupert, Ketchikan, Wrangel, Juneau and Skagway over the next four days before returning south. –Clinton Betz collection

The Princess Patricia...

"The *Princess Patricia* is giving us good satisfaction summer and winter, and is undoubtedly the best boat of her inches in this part of the world. She never would have been owned by the Canadian Pacific if it had not been for the talk you and I had concerning her the evening you spent with me in my house, because it was not until then that I had any confidence that she... had structural strength to make the sea voyage with safety."

> – Capt. Troup to Leslie Denny, Wm. Denny & Bros., December 19, 1913.

Clipping through the First Narrows into Burrard Inlet, the *Princess Pat* always left an impression of speed . The early turbine-powered steamer proved a shrewd purchase by Capt. Troup and she was a popular vessel on the Nanaimo service and for excursions. –Victor Lomas, RBCM

"PRINCESS"LINES

When the Duke of Connaught, the Governor-General of Canada, and his family toured British Columbia in 1912 the *Princess Alice* carried the vice-regal party to Prince Rupert which was then being developed as a major port by the Grand Trunk Pacific Railway. The Grand Trunk established a steamship service in competition with the CPR and built a trans-continental railway through northern British Columbia, the Canadian prairies and Ontario but went bankrupt and became a part of Canadian National Railways after the end of the First World War. The very new *Princess Alice*, with flags flying, was a pretty sight at the new city of Prince Rupert. In September 1919, the *Alice* would carry Edward, the Prince of Wales, between Vancouver and Victoria during his post-war tour of Canada. –AUTHOR'S COLLECTION

The Princess Maquinna...

"The *Maquinna* was designed and built specially for the West Coast of Vancouver Island trade, and should prove herself a splendid sea boat in plying this storm-battered coastline. The outstanding feature of the new craft is that all her decks, with the exception of the boat deck, are enclosed by the steel sides of the vessel, and the total absence of housework above the awning deck is a feature that cannot be duplicated by any other coastal vessel plying the Pacific."

–DAILY COLONIST, MAY 6, 1913.

Good intentions perhaps, but the CPR missed the point...

"They had no right to use that name Maquinna but they just took the name and they did not ask where the name came from. Nobody asked Maquinna for permission. The name Maquinna is more belonging to high ranking Hawiiha, what the Mamalthni [white people] call 'chiefs' and what we call Hawiiha. I care with a lot of feeling, knowing that I'm from the family of the Maquinnas of Mowachaht, handing down names through 'potlatch', as we call feasts and celebrations."

–CHIEF EARL MAQUINNA GEORGE, SPEAKING TO NANCY TURNER, AUGUST, 2000.

The *Princess Maquinna*, above left, shortly after her launching on December 24, 1912 at Esquimalt. The steamer *Tees*, shown at left, served the West Coast before the construction of the *Maquinna*. The West Coast was at once beautiful and unpredictable; it could be highly dangerous. The tranquil scene below, taken from the *Maquinna* shows the Canadian Northern cannery and dock at Uchucklesit. At right, the *Maquinna*, photographed by Cyril Littlebury, as she steamed past Stanley Park. –EARL MARSH COLLECTION; TWO PHOTOS, AUTHOR'S COLLECTION; AND DR. W. B. CHUNG COLLECTION, BELOW

Officers and senior personnel of the *Princess Maquinna* in September 1916: Capt. Edward Gillam is seated at centre, Purser Norman Taylor is standing at left and in front are Second Officer Leonard Thompson and Assistant Purser D. E. Horner. Unfortunately, the others are not identified. On May 3, 1929, Capt. Gillam was to die of an apparent heart attack on the *Princess Norah* off the West Coast. He had been with the Coast Service for 27 years. –R. Pocock photo, Norman Hacking collection, Vancouver Maritime Museum

Capt. Gillam and the Carelmapu..

On November 25, 1915, the Chilean barque *Carelmapu*, her sails torn away by a tremendous storm, was blown onto the rocks north of Ucluelet. Capt. Gillam took the *Maquinna* to her assistance. "Never... have I been called upon to nurse a ship through such terrible seas. The great seas were coming right over the pilot house and the spray was going right over the masthead. We ran the *Maquinna* right inside the first breakers and at one time were actually within 150 yards [about 140 m] of the *Carelmapu*... I brought the *Maquinna* to the wind and ordered oil to be pumped from the tanks and this precaution was effective in breaking up the seas...." Meanwhile the *Carelmapu* launched a boat and the *Maquinna* had let out a line to the stricken ship. "I had ordered the mate to let go the starboard anchor. We were in a most dangerous position as the seas were continually getting worse. Then the climax came. A thundering sea...came careening towards us.... The *Maquinna* rose on the sea, went back into the breakers and the windlass was wrecked. As she went up on the next sea the starboard anchor and chain still held but the seas were getting rapidly worse. Rather than have the bows torn out of her, I ordered the solid 1½-inch chain severed.... The *Carelmapu* was carried right over the reef by that sea and we saw nothing of the lifeboat containing the men. I was forced to take the *Maquinna* out to sea as we were fast being carried inshore. We steamed direct for Ucluelet and remained there overnight." Amazingly four men, including Capt. Desolmos, made it to shore but 19 others died.

—From Capt. Gillam's account in Victoria's *Daily Colonist*, Nov. 27, 1915. Photo from B.C. Archives, F-02230

The Princess Maquinna's West Coast...

On July 20, 1913, the *Princess Maquinna* sailed from Victoria on her first voyage, replacing the steamer *Tees* which had been on the route along the West Coast of Vancouver Island for many years. On July 28th, Capt. Troup wired Vice-President George Bury (later Sir George Bury) in Winnipeg that the "*Princess Maquinna*'s performance on her first trip to West Coast was very satisfactory in all particulars." On August 20, 1918, H. W. Brodie, the CPR's general passenger agent, made an inspection trip on the *Maquinna*.[15] Travel with Mr. Brodie from Victoria to Port Alice...

Victoria 11:00 p.m., August 20, 1918...
"She carried a full cargo, which included a partial deck load of lumber and machinery, also considerable iron piping and oil drums. There were about 50 Indians returning from Rivers Inlet canneries to their homes on the West Coast. They carry a large assortment of baggage, including blankets, mats, pots, pans and other cooking utensils. The entire family moves, including the smallest infant and the youngest dog. They take their position between decks, making themselves as comfortable as possible."

Port Renfrew...
"A heavy swell was running in the Straits and the majority of the passengers were quite ill."

Carmanah...
"This is a boat landing. We landed one passenger and floated ashore a small raft of lumber. The lumber is carefully lashed together and then dropped overboard and towed ashore by a row boat."

Clo-oose...
"We anchored at 9:26 a.m. There is a population of 60 whites and 40 Indians. The Nitinat cannery is situated here, and in 1917 had an output of 55,000 cases. The passengers are landed in small boats from the ship... very slow work. We did not weigh anchor until 11:00 a.m."

Bamfield...
"The Imperial Government Cable station and the Dominion Government Life Saving station are located here. We arrived at Bamfield at 1:15 p.m. The weather was thick with a drizzling rain and a long heavy swell, and the majority of the passengers were suffering from seasickness.... We landed a couple of passengers and some supplies for the station...."

Uchuchlesit...
"We arrived at 5:10 p.m. There is a population of about 100 whites, 75 Orientals and Indians. The cannery has four lines of machinery, two for canning herring and two for salmon. Each line has a record of 1,000 cases a day.... We were busy discharging cargo until 8:44 p.m...."

Port Alberni...
"We proceeded straight up the Alberni Canal to Port Alberni where we arrived at 10:45 p.m. A heavy rain was falling, it was very dark.... We unloaded a quantity of lumber and cast off at 0:53 a.m., Thursday morning, the 22nd. It is a very beautiful trip up the Alberni Canal...." After Alberni, the *Maquinna* called at Ecoole, Sechart, and Ucluelet.

Ucluelet...
We arrived at 7:23 a.m. and left at 8:57 a.m. There is a population of 40 whites and 60 Indians,

almost entirely made up of fishermen. Ucluelet is on the Northwestern side of Barclay Sound. It was very rough crossing over, and our passengers had a hard time of it once more. The weather throughout the entire morning was very thick, and it was necessary to use the ship's whistle constantly."

Tofino...

"Arrived at Tofino at 11:16 a.m. and left at 11:34 a.m. It has a population of 45 whites and 70 Indians. The Columbia Fisheries Ltd are operating here. A great deal of the business for the Clayoquot Sound Canning Co. is handled at this point. There is a regular Indian fishing village, with a general store. They have a large fleet of small gasoline fishing boats."

Clayoquot...

"Arrived at...11:51 a.m. and left at 2:47 p.m. A wharf landing. There is a long sandy beach, an old hotel and a general store. It is a typical Indian village. The Union Fisheries Co. are putting up a cold storage plant, which will have a capacity of about one million fish. It is a very pretty trip... passing through numerous islands... an inside passage all the way...."

Christie's School...

"This is an Indian School, and we landed nails and provisions...."

Ahousat [Ahousaht]...

"...we made a boat landing at 3:06 p.m. This is a very beautiful spot, the village being on a curved beach. The majority of our Indians disembarked. Dugouts... come along side of the ship, which anchors in the bay. The Indians pile into the dugouts, baggage, men, women, children ... and all sorts of paraphernalia.... It took about an hour." Then on to Sidney Inlet, Hesquiat, and Estevan Point.

Estevan...

"...we proceeded out in the open, past Estevan Point, where there is a light, which we passed at 9:41 p.m. The weather was very thick and we were obliged to use our whistle continuously. The ship was headed directly for Nootka Sound [and] Yuquot Light House. There is a hand fog signal at this lighthouse.... We had very considerable difficulty in picking up the light and finally succeeded about 11:17 p.m. and ran away into Nootka, where we tied up at 11:46 p.m., remaining there for the night and leaving there at 7:19 a.m. Friday."

Nootka...

"At Nootka a large cannery has been established. There is a population of about 60 Indians and three whites in the village and then at the cannery there would be over 60 whites and 40 or more Indians and Orientals.... In 1917 the cannery put up 45,000 cases of salmon and 10,000 cases canned herring and pilchards....

"On leaving Nootka we proceeded out of the Sound and headed Northwest, skirting the Coast. The weather though fine was quite rough, and the passengers once more became violently ill.

"Proceeding North, we made a long trip, passing Esperanza Inlet and on to Kyuquot Sound, where we quickly ran into the protection of the sheltering islands, and passed up the sound to Narrow Cut Creek, where the Kyuquot Whaling station is located... we tied up... at 12:40."

[Southbound, the *Maquinna* returned for nine hours to load 3,700 cases of pilchards for Vancouver.]

The *Maquinna* wove her way in and out of the deep coastal inlets of Vancouver Island's West Coast, stopping at remote canneries, logging camps, mines, First Nation villages and other settlements. At left, she is at the Nootka Sound cannery. Boat landings were common: a Nuu-Chah-Nulth man maneuvers his cedar dugout canoe close to the steamer and, below, at Ahousaht people return home from work at the canneries at Rivers Inlet. Below right, the primitive Jeune Landing wharf of the Coast Copper Company against the dense forest backdrop so typical of the West Coast. –Dr. W. B. Chung collection

Kyuquot...

"The population of the whaling station consists of about 20 whites and 30 or more Indians. It is operated by the Victoria Whaling Co. They are canning the whale meat this year, and have a capacity of 2,000 cases a day. They put up fertilizer and whale oil.... Everything in connection with the whale is utilized. The most indescribable stench prevails at the whaling station...."

Kyuquot Village...

"We made a boat landing at 5:43 p.m., sending ashore in numerous boats the balance of our Indian passengers. The village has a population of about 4 whites and 35 Indians. There is a spruce logging camp in operation which employs about 60 men.... At 6:43 p.m. we weighed anchor and started for the open sea, and soon ran into a brisk head wind and a heavy sea." Then the *Maquinna* steamed on past Solander Island, "one of the finest sights on the Pacific Coast," and to Brooks Bay, Quatsino, Jeune Landing and finally Port Alice....

Port Alice...

"...has a population of considerably over 600 whites. The Whalen Pulp & Paper Mills Ltd have erected their plant at this port, also a saw mill.... The Whalen people practically control the whole place. They have their own cottages for the men, their own store, and run the Post Office. We landed at Port Alice 58 through passengers. The total distance from Victoria to Port Alice is 424 miles [682 km], and of this the steamer travels in the open sea about 169 miles [272 km], which would be about 15 hours steaming in open water. We were given a big send off by the entire population who came to the wharf, sang songs and made a great fuss over the departure of the ship, because they will not see another one for some ten days."

Overall, 141 first class and 53 deck class passengers were carried for a total of $1,530.20 in revenue and 314.75 tons of freight produced $3,626.30. Southbound, the route was retraced to Victoria and the *Maquinna* carried 164 cabin passengers and 24 deck passengers for revenue of $1,519.25 and 162.75 tons of freight for a return of $921.30. Total revenue for the round trip was $7,592.15.

A War Bride on the West Coast...

Dorothy Abraham came to the West Coast in 1919 as a young war bride from England. She made her new home with her husband on Vargas Island and later at Tofino. "Late at night," she wrote, "we boarded the *Princess Maquinna*...a ship which came to mean much to me in my years on the Coast; and we set off on the last lap of our journey to the longed-for, much-talked-of, Home in the West. I was getting very excited. My husband's place was on an open beach, beautiful, rugged, terrifyingly lonely, with a little wooden shack, about two miles through dense bush from my in-laws...." The *Maquinna* became Dorothy's lifeline with the outside world for many years to come and an inextricable part of her memoir *Lone Cone, Life on the West Coast of Vancouver Island* published in 1945. "Lest my tales of rough weather and seasickness put you off this fascinating West Coast," she mused, "let me say that seasickness is like the West Coast rain, the moment it is over you forget all about it... afterall, all life is always full of ups and downs, especially aboard ship."

Dorothy Abraham, at left, seated on the deck of the *Maquinna,* with warmly dressed travelling companions, all with knitting in hand to help pass the time. The views at right, from Dorothy Abraham's album, show the *Maquinna* at Tofino. –F. V. Longstaff photo, left, all Author's collection

Suddenly the piano playing stopped...

"A bunch of loggers, their wives and young unmarried men, clambered aboard; they had been drinking. In the alleged saloon on the *Maquinna* was about a three-quarter keyboard piano, not far from my stateroom. That piano had weathered as many storms as the *Maquinna* had, and it was terribly out of tune, but that gang got that piano hooked up, and they were dancing and laughing and talking. We had cast off and had turned around and were heading out of Nootka Sound; we had to go outside, until we passed Estevan Point. These guys were whooping it up and playing this little piano for all it would stand.... Within five minutes after we stuck our nose outside, they were GONE. No more piano, no more laughter, no more gaiety. It was all over. The Captain later told me that we were having gusts up to 80 miles [130 km] an hour and it was blowing between 50 and 60 knots steadily outside."

—Lester Arellanes, recalling a West Coast voyage.

The Tidewater Copper Company's Indian Chief Mine at Stewardson Inlet in Clayoquot Sound, photographed from the *Princess Maquinna* in 1919. –C.W. Hamilton photo, Ken Gibson collection

Miniature Liners of the Pacific Coast

ONE REASON THE CPR STEAMSHIPS RESEMBLED MINIATURE LINERS rather than ferry boats was that they were built to operate periodically in very rough water. In winter, when gales came in from the Pacific, conditions could get very stormy particularly off Trial Island near Victoria, while crossing Juan de Fuca Strait on the Seattle route and in the open waters of the Strait of Georgia. In November 1904, Capt. Troup made the following report to Arthur Piers, Manager of Canadian Pacific Steamship Lines in Montreal:

> On Saturday morning, the 19th instant, we had a vicious south-east gale on the coast. It struck Victoria about midnight, and as the *Princess Victoria* sailed at 2 o'clock a.m. she went out into the teeth of it. There was a very heavy sea running off Discovery Island, and ... Capt. Griffin reports she jumped into the sea pretty hard, and in fact put her nose under and drenched things somewhat forward. No damage was done, but on account of the way she was pitching and some racing going on [when the propellers came partly above the water] he had to slow her down. On our course this run is such that we head the sea until we pass Discovery Island, then we have the sea on the quarter. On the night in question, shortly after he hauled her round she took a sea over that low bulwark outside of the dining room aft and filled herself full. Everything had been made snug, however; slat shutters were up in front of the dining room windows and no damage occurred. Capt. Griffin says there was no fault to be found with her steering that night, when he gave her the helm she came round nicely, that her rolling when in the trough of the sea was not excessive, and when before the sea she ran nicely. She will rarely ever get worse weather than the night in question, and I think we need have no fears of her whatever so long as reasonably good judgment is used in ballasting and handling of her.
>
> The *Princess Beatrice* crossed over to Port Townsend in the same blow, and it is needless to say that she made fine weather of it.

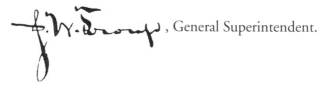

, General Superintendent.

While Capt. Griffin was undoubtedly exhilarated by the experience, and Capt. Troup envious of the challenge, passengers may not have shared Troup's enthusiasm for the *Victoria's* ability to handle the rough weather. On board, those less accustomed to the sea may have

Passengers disembark from a new *Princess Charlotte* at Victoria with a newly-opened Empress Hotel in the background. At right, the passengers enjoy the *Charlotte's* open decks on a beautiful day during the Second World War — AUTHOR'S COLLECTION; WALTON BARNES PHOTO, JACK LENFESTY COLLECTION

Remembering the Princess Victoria...

"The officers, crew and stewards and all others who served on the ship absorbed from her an esprit seldom equalled. Passengers came under the influence when they walked up the gang plank. In such circumstances manners improved and courtesy and consideration were in the very atmosphere.

One summer evening in 1907 my wife and I boarded the *Victoria* just as her lines were being cast off for the night run to Vancouver. We had no stateroom reservation but trusted to luck. Our luck ran out. There was no space available. The purser was explaining to us that my wife could have a berth in a women's cabin and a cot would be set up for me in one of the passageways. We must have shown our disappointment because as we turned away from the window a young man touched me on the arm and said, 'I couldn't help hearing your talk with the purser. I have a stateroom and I'm alone. I hope you and your wife will accept it.' He brushed aside protests and turned over the key.

That act was probably not typical because the man who did it was far from ordinary, but it did happen on the *Princess Victoria* where all those who came aboard felt they were guests."

— EARL MARSH'S COLLECTION, PERHAPS WRITTEN BY H. C. JAMES, GENERAL PASSENGER AGENT, VANCOUVER, IN 1952.

been more concerned with the states of their stomachs. Shaky photographs show waves breaking well over the decks and cabins of rolling *Princesses* struggling around Trial Island in weather that would have held a later generation of ferries in port waiting for the storms to abate. Good sea boats that they were, the *Princesses* seldom stayed in port in the face of a gale in the Straits or for winter winds and storms blowing out of the Gulf of Alaska.

Although the CPR and other shipping companies placed great importance on the speed of their vessels, in truth they were seldom operated at their highest speeds for simple reasons of economy. The *Princess Victoria* burned an estimated 20 or 21 tons of coal a day to steam at 12 knots (13.8 miles or 22.25 km an hour), the economical speed she averaged on her delivery voyage to Victoria, but to reach 18.5 knots (21.25 miles or 34.3 km an hour), coal consumption rose dramatically to 120 tons a day. Speed was important for publicity purposes and it also permitted the steamers to make up time if there were delays anywhere along their routes, but speed was expensive and at sustained levels was hard on the steamers.[16]

Despite the arrival of new vessels and the expansion of services along the Pacific Coast, the *Princess Victoria* continued to maintain an unsurpassed record of achievement. In May, 1911, Chief Engineer A. Wallace reported to Capt. P. J. Hickey, the *Victoria's* master, that she had steamed the equivalent of more than four times around the world in just over a year. Between March 7, 1910 and May 23, 1911, she steamed over 100,000 nautical miles (115,000 miles or 185,000 km). During that time–443 days–she averaged 326 nautical miles (375 miles or 600 km) a day and was only off the run for three days. This impressive record on the Triangle Run, running seven days each week, included port time, bunkering about 60 tons of coal a day, handling baggage and mail and package freight, and carrying thousands of passengers. Under the headlines "May be a World's Steaming Record," the *Colonist* concluded that "if there is any other steamer in any part of the world doing more faithful service, the officers of the *Princess Victoria* and the officials of the Canadian Pacific Railway company would like to hear it."[17]

By 1912, the CPR was converting its coastal steamers to burn oil for fuel instead of coal. The conversions required the installation of oil bunkers, fuel pumps, oil burning apparatus and changes to the furnaces of the boilers but the results were gratifying for the company. Crew sizes were reduced and oil was a cleaner and more efficient fuel. Messy and time consuming bunkering, the dumping of ashes, and the annoyance of soot and ash that could blow all over the decks, cabins and, most importantly, the passengers, were all but eliminated. Fuel costs for the *Princess Victoria*, including reduced fuel and reductions in crew, dropped from $19,662 to $18,150, saving $1,512 a month, while for the large *Princess Charlotte* the monthly costs decreased from $23,880 to $22,470 for a net saving of $1,410.[18]

Onboard the Princesses

"When weary of the petty rounds of irritating concerns you need an outing around the Triangle, an ocean trip on smooth waters among the islands with salt air," CPR advertising extolled in 1910.

Voyages on the *Princesses* were exciting adventures. In these views, the *Princess Victoria* passes another *Princess* and William A. and Ellen Sharp enjoy the sunshine on the *Charlotte*, below, and on the *Vic*, centre right, about 1912. "The photographer was being naughty," she penned on the back of the photo. At right, Anita Hayward posing in an officer's uniform on the *Princess Sophia* on September 20, 1912. Crowds fill the decks of the *Charlotte* and the *Victoria*, far right. –AUTHOR'S COLLECTION EXCEPT VMM, 4043, FAR RIGHT

PRINCESS VICTORIA

Dressed in spotless, pressed uniforms, hair combed and meticulously parted, the members of the *Princess Alice's* catering department, including two stewardesses, posed for their group portrait at Victoria about 1913. George Woollett was Chief Steward at this time. Soon many of these young men would be joining the army and going off to war in Europe. Crews were kept busy on the tight schedules maintained by the steamers during the busy seasons. Stewards had to make up overnight cabins, serve meals and snacks, wash dishes, polish silver and clean the lounges and dining room on a schedule that left little time for leisure. Gary Richardson recalled his first summer as a steward. "The morning of the first day that I worked I nearly passed out before lunch. Then I got used to it and never looked back. After that I was constantly tired to the point I could even go to bed at lunch for 20 minutes and fall fast asleep, but one of my buddies would awaken me and away we would go again." Daytime sailings on the Triangle Service were usually four and a half hours. The overnight trips normally departed between 11:00 and midnight and arrived about breakfast time the next day. —AUTHOR'S COLLECTION

At right, the *Princess Patricia*, with an escort of gulls, slices through calm seas as she enters Burrard Inlet. As an excursion steamer, the *Pat* was ever popular as these two young men, with their straw "boaters" demonstrate. At far right, Carl F. Timms captured this scene that he called "The Parting at the Dock," with the *Charlotte* at Vancouver in the early 1900s. —CANADIAN PACIFIC ARCHIVES; AUTHOR'S COLLECTION AND VANCOUVER PUBLIC LIBRARY, 2970

÷ "The Parting at the Dock" ÷

VANCOUVER

When the Troops Went off to War...

In the fateful summer of 1914 the First World War began in Europe. On August 4th, Great Britain and Canada, whose foreign policy then was still tied to Britain's, were at war with Germany and her Allies. Canada was quick to mobilize its forces and by late 1914 the Canadian Expeditionary Force numbered 50,000 men. Quiet Victoria became a major base for training as more and more young men volunteered amid a wave of optimism and national pride. "They would be home by Christmas" was the popular opinion, however unrealistic it was. Thousands of troops were carried by the steamers to Victoria for training and back to Vancouver where they boarded special trains to take them east and ultimately to the Western Front. Juggling regular schedules with troop movements could tax the limits of the fleet. Often over 1000 men with their equipment would board the waiting steamers, crowding the decks to the point where it looked as if the ships might tip over. Sometimes additional lifesaving equipment had to be found to meet legal requirements. *Princesses* also brought contingents from coastal communities and the Yukon to Victoria and Vancouver. Several steamers could be used to handle the larger movements of troops.

The *Princess Sophia* with every inch of her decks crowded with troops leaves Victoria and above, the *Princess Adelaide* pulls away with about 300 men heading for the Western Front. On the *Adelaide* are likely troops of the 2nd Contingent of the Canadian Expeditionary Force that left Victoria on February 14, 1915. Thousands of people lined the route of march to the docks and crowded the piers to give the men a rousing and emotional send-off. "Never has such profound emotion moved a Victoria throng as dominated the multitude..." noted *The Daily Colonist*. —EARL J. MARSH COLLECTION; ELWOOD WHITE COLLECTION

The beginning of the First World War in 1914 ended immediate plans for expanding the fleet and the *Princesses* continued their services largely uninterrupted by the war in Europe. The diversion of the new *Princess Margaret* and *Princess Irene* to military service was disappointing but the *Vic* and *Charlotte* were still modern and effective vessels so the service was largely unaffected.

The war years were emotional times climaxed by the movement of troops, described at left, and the perils of navigation along the Northwest Coast, which as Capt. Troup was all too well aware, could be uncompromisingly harsh. On August 26, 1914, the *Princess Victoria* collided with the Admiral Line's *Admiral Sampson* in dense fog off Point No Point in Puget Sound. In just 15 minutes the *Sampson* sank with a loss of 16 lives. Worse was to come. At 2:10 a.m., October, 24, 1918, just days before the Armistice, the *Princess Sophia* ran hard aground on Vanderbilt Reef in the Lynn Canal, a long and deep mountain-walled inlet that was the shipping route to Skagway. Stuck fast on the reef, at first the steamer seemed safe and it looked as if she could be floated free on the next high tide, but this was not to be. Although several small vessels were close by, the weather conditions were rough, the water penetratingly-cold and Capt. Louis P. Locke decided that his passengers were safer on board. It is possible that the passengers might have been taken off, but likely with loss of life and Capt. Locke fatefully decided to wait in hopes that the weather would moderate. Wireless messages reached Victoria and Capt. Troup immediately dispatched the *Princess Alice* to pick up the passengers and the *Tees* to assist with getting the *Sophia* off the reef.

She remained stranded through that day and night but the weather worsened and by late afternoon on the 25th., the smaller vessels, still standing by, had to retreat. That evening, in the midst of a horrible storm, the *Princess* was swept clear of the reef and sank with everyone on board. Officially there were 343 people on the *Sophia* but it is likely that as many as 353 people were onboard; it seems we will never know. Not one person survived although two men reached shore but died of exposure. Only a dog, who swam to shore, survived.

The loss of the *Sophia,* "through the perils of the sea," as the official inquiry concluded, was a devastating blow to the Coast Service and to people in the Yukon and all along the Pacific Coast.[19] Capt. Troup was heartsick over the loss, and the subsequent inquiries and lawsuits continued for many years. The only settlements were for members of the crew whose families received worker's compensation payments. In the end, neither the CPR nor Capt. Locke was found to be legally responsible for the loss of the ship. With no survivors and the tragedy rife for second-guessing over what might have happened, controversy continued for decades. In the end, the North Coast, so beautiful and yet so treacherous, had claimed another ship and little could be done but mourn the loss.

The *Princess Sophia*, above, at Skagway in 1918 not long before her loss and below, stranded on Vanderbilt Reef, about 10 hours after running hard aground on the high tide. —EARL MARSH COLLECTION; WINTER-POND PHOTO, AUTHOR'S COLLECTION

"*Princess Sophia*" ten hours after striking Vanderbilt Reef. Winter-Pond Juneau

#52.

The Sad Story Unfolded...

"*Sophia* ashore Vanderbilt Reef, send all possible help." —SOS FROM THE *Princess Sophia* 2:15 AM, OCTOBER 24, 1918.

The Northwest Coast was remote, and wireless messages were slow, relayed through shore stations and so frustratingly brief. The *Sophia's* wireless operator, David H. Robinson, did his best to communicate with F.F.W. Lowle, CPR's agent in Juneau, and Capt. Troup. They convey some of the frustration and helplessness as events unfolded...

32 FAB 36 RADIO   S.S. *Princess Sophia*   October 24th 1918
Troup, Victoria, B.C.
The *Princess Sophia* ran on Vanderbilt Reef, Lynn Canal, at 3:00 o'clock. Ship not taking any water, unable to back off at high water, fresh northerly wind, ship pounded, assistance on way from Juneau. Locke. 9:11 a.m.

RUSH   Oct. 24th, 1918,   F.F.W. Lowle, Juneau, Alaska.
Send all possible assistance to *Sophia*. Advise as to what you have been able to do for passengers.   J. W. Troup.   10:20 a.m.

125 EAR 32 RADIO VIA SITKA, ALAS. & SEATTLE, WN.
S.S. Princess Sophia, Juneau, Alas.   October 24th, 1918
Troup, Victoria, B.C.
Sophia fast on reef, resting safely, strong northerly wind, unable to transfer passengers until wind moderates or perhaps at high water, steamer *Peterson* and two gas boats standing by. Locke.

4:32 p.m. Victoria, B.C.   October 25th, 1918
F. F. W. Lowle, Juneau Alaska.
You have not replied to my wires. Please make every effort get suitable boats to *Sophia* for transferring passengers moment it is safe. *Alice* should arrive Juneau Saturday night.   J. W. Troup

From U.S. Steamer *Cedar*, via U.S.A.T. *Burnside*   Oct. 26th, 1918
Been standing by since 7:00 p.m. on 24th but impossible get near enough to do anything account heavy northerly gale and big seas. *Cedar* got within four hundred yards of her yesterday a.m. but anchors would not hold and sea and wind drove her away late night. *Sophia* told them they were foundering. *Cedar* made full speed to her in blinding snow storm but could not find her....

To Capt. Troup. Juneau to Bremerton Navy Yard   October 26th 1918
Princess Sophia driven across reef last night. No survivors.... Everything possible done here to help. Nothing could be done owing to terrible rough weather. Radio, Juneau. 14:38. received.

Even in wartime gray, the *Princess Margaret* retained the familiar lines which would have made her a beautiful addition to the fleet. –Dr. W. B. Chung collection

The Fate of the Princess Margaret...

"The general design and dimensions of the *Princess Margaret* suggest that she would be in no way out of fashion or obsolete when she went into service. The design was our own.... The form of the vessel... is beautiful and cannot be improved upon at the present day."

> –Capt. Troup to Vice President D. C. Coleman, October 5, 1927.

Although she could have been reconditioned for about $1,000,000, Capt. Troup and Capt. Neroutsos could not see how she could cover costs on the summer-only Alaska service. All other routes for which she was suited were served well by existing ships. With reluctance, the CPR declined to purchase the *Margaret*.

"Have your *Princess Margaret* built 1914 for sale. Will you make an offer. Can get her great bargain."

> –Cable from Thos. McLaren & Co. Steamship brokers, Glasgow, to Capt. C.D. Neroutsos, April 13, 1929.

"Your cable. No longer interested in *Princess Margaret*."

> –Capt. Neroutsos to Thos. McLaren, April 13, 1929.

The Princess Irene and the Princess Margaret...

The *Princess Irene* and *Princess Margaret* would have been the largest and fastest steamships on the Pacific Coast but they never joined the Coast Steamship Service. With 202 staterooms providing berths for 423 passengers and dining rooms with seating for 186 they were luxuriously appointed. Built by the Wm. Denny & Bros. yards at Dumbarton, the *Margaret* was launched on June 24, 1914 and the *Irene* followed on October 20. At 5900 gross tons, 395 feet (120 m) in length and 54 feet (16.5 m) in breadth, they were not exceeded in size until the *Princess of Nanaimo* surpassed them in tonnage and the *Princess of Vancouver* in length. Both steamers were used as minelayers. The *Margaret* was charted between December 26, 1914 and April 27, 1919 and was then sold to the Admiralty, finally being scrapped in 1929. The *Irene's* charter began on January 20, 1915 but she blew up at Sheerness on May 27, 1915, with the loss of approximately 270 crew and dockyard workmen. A monument at Sheerness commemorates those who lost their lives on the *Irene* and also on HMS *Bulwark* in 1914. The CPR did well from the charters which returned more than was invested in the steamers. With lowered expectations for post-war travel, Capt. Troup and CPR management concluded reluctantly that smaller vessels would be a better investment for the Coast Service and developed designs that ultimately became the *Princess Kathleen* and *Princess Marguerite*. The *Margaret* and *Irene* had been developed in a time of enormous expansion and optimism amid worries about competition from the Grand Trunk and the Canadian Northern railways.

Halcyon Years
& the Depression

❧

"The Victoria *has been a wonder, she has been the backbone of the fleet for years, and she must not give way to any newcomer in the family."*

–Capt. James W. Troup, quoted on board the new *Princess Kathleen*, May 1925.

"There are many complaints made by motorists on account of the difficulty and time occupied in stowing their cars on board the Princess Patricia, *having to turn and twist in awkward places in order to get them on. There is also the old trouble of having to lower the tops of open cars, loaded on the SS* Princess Patricia *on account of the low clearance."*

–H. J. Maguire to Capt. Troup, August 27, 1925.

".... at 4:00 p.m., the good ship Maquinna *was at Tofino northbound."*[20]

–Earle Kelly, "Mr. Good Evening," on the Vancouver *Province's* 8:00 p.m. newscast on radio station cjor.

The beautiful *Princess Kathleen* at Seattle, the city she would come to know so well on the famed Triangle Route. –Clinton Betz

CHAPTER 2

Prosperous Times and New Ships

THE 1920S WERE THE SECOND GOLDEN DAYS of the B.C. Coast Steamship Service. James Troup remained as manager and guided the service through another period of rapid expansion and modernization that culminated in the construction of seven new *Princess* steamships and the addition of several smaller vessels including a pioneering diesel-powered automobile ferry. It was a decade of prosperity, growth and optimism.

The first new vessel to join the fleet after the end of the First World War was the *Princess Louise*, a replacement for the *Princess Sophia*. Enlarged and improved over her predecessor, the *Louise* was a fine, well-built vessel constructed in North Vancouver at the Wallace Yards. Powered by a conventional triple-expansion engine, she was ordered from the Wallace Yards because the builders in Scotland were fully booked with orders replacing tonnage lost or worn out during the First World War. Later Capt. Troup and CPR management considered more construction at local yards but they were skeptical about the experience of the British Columbia builders in constructing the first-class steamers with turbine propulsion desired for the service and the most competitive bids came from the yards in Britain.

Troup and the Coast Service staff were at work on many projects to keep up with the rapidly changing conditions on the coast, the growth in traffic and the need to replace older units of the fleet. The Nanaimo service and the growing demand for carrying automobiles to Vancouver Island were an increasing concern, as were the limited terminal facilities in Victoria. Traffic between Vancouver and Nanaimo grew from just over 11,000 passengers in 1917 to nearly 147,000 in 1923 and automobile revenues increased from just over $500 to over $33,000 in the same period.

The rise in automobile traffic led to the construction of the last wooden vessel added to the fleet, the diesel-powered *Motor Princess*, built in Esquimalt by Yarrows, which had taken over the Bullen yards at the time the *Princess Maquinna* was under construction. Planning included experiments at the National Physical Laboratory, Teddington, England, during 1922 and by the end of the year after several proposals were considered, Yarrows was given the contract for $240,000, which was substantially less than the cost of a steel-hulled vessel.

The *Motor Princess*, with the exception of her wooden construction, was an innovative vessel for the Coast Service. The keel was laid on January 10, 1923, and 97 working days later the ferry, built of local Douglas-fir and the hull steel-reinforced, was delivered to the

The Princess Louise...

The *Louise* was the largest coastal steamship built in British Columbia for the Canadian Pacific and she filled the gap left by the loss of the *Princess Sophia* on the Alaska service as well as being a valuable relief steamer on the Triangle Route. Built at the Wallace Shipbuilding & Dry Dock Company in North Vancouver, she was christened by Mrs. Troup on August 29, 1921. Accompanying her, in the photo above, was D. C. Coleman, Vice-President, Western Lines. In 1942 Coleman succeeded Sir Edward Beatty as CPR president and in 1943 became president and chairman. At right, the steamer slides down the ways to the cheers of an appreciative crowd. The 330-foot (100-m) steamer was powered by a single, four-cylinder, triple-expansion steam engine with 28, 43, 50 and 50-inch diameter cylinders and a stroke of 39 inches. With steam provided by four Scotch Marine boilers, her contract speed was 16 knots. The *Princess Louise* was built to the CPR's high standards of accommodations and provided 110 staterooms with 232 beds or berths. In addition, there were 22 standee (dormitory-style) bunks in second class. Dining room seating was 100. Her normal crew was about 80: 17 in the Deck Department; 14 in the Engine Department; 45 in the Steward's Department and 4 pursers. Her passenger license was for 1000 people. Capt. Andrew Slater was her first master.

The *Princess Louise*, at left, backs away from the Victoria docks in a beautiful portrait by Maurice Chandler on August 13, 1940. –AUTHOR'S COLLECTION; MILTON BRALEY COLLECTION, TWO PHOTOS THIS PAGE

The Motor Princess...
"She is giving us entire satisfaction and shows good economy....
I would not say that her handling in and out of dock is as satisfactory as a steam plant for the reason that the McIntosh & Seymour
engines...will not turn slower than about 125 revolutions...hence
when maneuvering around in close quarters, allowance must be
made for very considerable movement back and forth. The
engines...do not respond quite as promptly as a steam engine;
sometimes there is a little wait for the movement of the engine after
the telegraph rang."

—Capt. Troup to W. W. Mills, June 9, 1923.

The *Motor Princess* was a significant departure in design from the CPR's other *Princess* vessels. Functional and business-like, she was a well-built and serviceable vessel and the first major automobile ferry to operate in British Columbia. Fares on the CPR vessels varied with the size of the automobile. Between Nanaimo and Vancouver vehicles were carried for $4.00 to $6.00 while on the longer Seattle-to-Victoria and Vancouver-to-Victoria routes fares were between $5.00 and $7.00. Driver and passenger fares were extra. Early terminals, like the Sidney dock above, were primitive but effective for driving cars on and off the *Motor Princess*. – Maurice Chandler, above left, and Author's collection

CPR. The ferry, which was powered by twin diesel engines, could carry 32 automobiles on the main deck and 13 on the upper deck, accessible by a ramp, and was constructed so that in the winter months the *Motor Princess* could operate in freight service to the North Coast. Passenger accommodations included two observation rooms, and a coffee shop-dining room, with maple flooring, suitable for dancing. For many years the *Motor Princess* was to be the only diesel-powered vessel in the B.C. Coast Steamship fleet.

The intention was to place her in a summer service between Bellingham, Washington, and Sidney on Vancouver Island, through the beautiful San Juan Islands. The route was sheltered and the 170-foot (51.8-m) ferry, which was designed for a maximum speed of about 14 knots (16 miles or 26 km an hour), could make the trip in about 3 hours and 15 minutes. Service began on May 23, 1923. However, the route was not very profitable and was maintained in part to discourage other shipping companies from entering the trade to Vancouver Island from the Seattle area. In May 1926 the *Motor Princess* was reassigned to the Vancouver-to-Nanaimo summer route, providing a three-hour crossing time, and making two round trips each day, except Sundays, while the *Princess Pat* made two trips each way, daily except Sunday, making the trips in just 2 hours and 15 minutes. This service continued through the summer of 1928 and the arrival of the new *Princess Elaine*. Before the *Motor Princess* was transferred to the Vancouver-to-Nanaimo service, the old *Charmer* was used to supplement the *Princess Patricia* with somewhat mixed results pending the construction of a new vessel for the route.

Rattenbury Designs the New Victoria Terminal, 1923...

"I would be more than delighted to design this building. The Panorama, on entering Victoria, is so unique - with the Embankment - Green Sward - Empress Hotel, and the Parliament Buildings - and so much of it is my life's work that I would put my whole heart into designing a building that would harmonize and add to the beauty of the surroundings.

Following on your suggestion, that I should submit a proposal for making complete working plans, detail plans, heating plans, electrical plans and specifications, together with obtaining tenders and letting contracts (but not including supervision of construction). I am willing to do the above work for 3 1/2 p.c. on the cost of the building - which I understand to be $175,000. and my fee is to be based on above amount only. And I undertake to obtain Tender at above amount (within 10% margin)."

–F. M. Rattenbury, Architect, to Capt. J. W. Troup, May 1, 1923.

The impressive terminal building at Victoria was built of cast stone, composed of concrete, sand and gravel mixed on site, and the sills were of granite from Nelson Island in the entrance to Jervis Inlet. The plinth course was made of limestone from Newcastle Island, near Nanaimo, and the roof was covered in Welsh slate and a polished marble base extended around all of the corridors, waiting rooms and other public areas. Maritime theme decorations were applied to the building including the one above over the entrance on Belleville Street. The main waiting room, with a large, decorative open fireplace, a 17-foot (5.2-m) ceiling and floor laid with stone from Haddington Island in Broughton Strait, a ladies' waiting room and a smoking room with terrazzo flooring, and ticket offices occupied the main floor at street level. The rest of the building was used as offices. Earl Marsh, to whom this book is dedicated, at right, with William Hillier and Shirley Hayhurst, from the headquarters staff are pictured in the 1940s. *Princesses* crowd the Victoria docks, at right, beside the new terminal in the 1920s. From left, are the *Adelaide*, the freighter *Nootka*, the *Alice*, *Charlotte* and *Marguerite* or *Kathleen*. –Earl Marsh collection, and Vancouver Maritime Museum

Meanwhile, terminal and office facilities in Victoria were increasingly inadequate by the early 1920s. According to Capt. Troup, by 1922 "the place is no longer fit for occupancy, and extensive repairs must be undertaken before the building literally falls down."[21] The alternative, adopted by the company at Capt. Troup's recommendation, was to hire Francis Rattenbury to design a new structure that would prove to be a permanent and enduring monument to the B.C. Coast Service. Rattenbury, famous for his design of the Parliament Buildings, opened in 1898, and CPR's landmark Empress Hotel, completed in 1908, was the ideal choice for the project.

Rattenbury's proposal complemented the other major buildings around Victoria's compact Inner Harbour beautifully. "I feel that you will like the design," he wrote Troup. "The long horizontal lines, with the Ionic Colonnade, will make a dignified entrance to the City - simple and strong in outline. There are so many Towers and Minarets in the Parliament Buildings and Empress that to introduce features of this kind into a small building would be a mistake...."[22]

As he promised, Rattenbury delivered his building designs and the contract was completed by the Luney Brothers well within budget and to the satisfaction of the CPR. Measuring 122 feet by 54 feet (37 m by 16.5 m), the building was four storeys high. It was described as "classical design of the Greek Ionic order, with wide pylons fluting the two principal facades. The ionic columns are surmounted by bold cornice and entablature."[23] It became a landmark of Victoria's harbour that would fulfill Rattenbury's wish to have a structure to complement his other masterpieces around the harbour.

Vancouver Piers...

Vancouver developed as a major port after the completion of the Canadian Pacific Railway in 1885. In 1889, the tracks were extended along Burrard Inlet to Vancouver and shipping facilities soon followed. The early docks, with freight sheds and passenger facilities, were built parallel to the railway yards and the harbour front. Coastal and deep sea ships docked there routinely but, by the early 1900s, the capacity was strained. The CPR's Pier A was built out into the harbour in 1908 and additions and improvements were made in 1912 and 1913. A major new home for the Coast Service in Vancouver was completed in 1913 with the construction of Pier D at the foot of Granville Street, 400 feet (120 m) long and nearly 150 feet (46 m) wide. This structure soon became inadequate and it was expanded in 1917 and 1918 by 600 feet (183 m) in length and widened to 160 feet (49 m). The expanded pier was built on fill dredged from the harbour, and on pilings up to 125 feet (38 m) long using a pile driver thought to be one of the largest in the world. Two railway tracks were laid to within 100 feet (30 m) of the end of the pier and a huge wooden-framed shed enclosed the structure. Sydney E. Junkins & Co. were the principal contractors and the work was supervised by John G. Sullivan, the CPR's Chief Engineer for Western Lines.[24]

As CPR services expanded in the 1920s, and with the arrival of new *Empress* liners and *Princesses*, port facilities in Vancouver again became overcrowded and in 1921 a new pier was authorized. Pier B-C, 1,120 feet (341 m) long and 350 feet (107 m) wide, was built to the west of Pier D. With an estimated cost of $4,000,000, the massive structure was built on reinforced concrete piles and harbour fill and featured elevated road access to the upper levels with railway tracks entering the lower levels of the sheds. Opened on July 4, 1927, it was used primarily by the *Empresses*, the Canadian-Australasian Line's *Aorangi* and *Niagara*, and other ocean shipping, leaving Pier D for the *Princesses*. Nonetheless, the *Princess Louise* was the first vessel to tie up at the new pier and her captain, Arthur Slater, was presented with a silk hat and a gold-headed cane to mark the occasion. The north and west sides were intended primarily for the coastal steamers and the east side was used by the *Empress* liners. Pier D burned on July 27, 1938 and after that the *Princesses* moved to the new Pier B-C, sharing facilities with the ocean steamships. Pier B-C was demolished in the 1980s to make way for Canada Place built for Vancouver's Expo 86 and to provide a new facility for cruise ships.[25]

Pier D, shown on September 10, 1926, at left, was easily accessible by automobile and the ticketing areas were functional and spacious. The extended pier gave ample room for the growing *Princess* fleet including the *Alice*, at left, and the *Maquinna* and *Patricia*, above, all photographed on September 15, 1928.

The Canadian Pacific's magnificent trans-Pacific liner, the *Empress of Japan,* below left, at Pier B-C on December 5, 1937 with the Canadian Australasian Line's *Aorangi* in the background. At far left, the new Pier B-C in 1928. Below, the fire that destroyed Pier D nearly caught the *Princess Charlotte*. The *Alice* is at left.
–ALBERT H. PAULL PHOTOS, AUTHOR'S COLLECTION; INTERIOR VIEW AND FIRE, VANCOUVER MARITIME MUSEUM

Troup's hand was everywhere...

"Troup supervised the design of the whole darn works, the stair-wells, the balcony and that sort of thing. He created that design. Once you got into one of the ships, the basic design was the same, even on the B.C. Lake & River Service."

–EARL J. MARSH, BCCSS ACCOUNTANT AND HISTORIAN.

The Excellence of the ships...

"Our experience has been that traffic grows with the excellence of the ships. The better the steamers, the greater the travel. That's our policy as well as our experience, and I think the people of Victoria, from their own experience, can testify to its soundness."

– CAPT. JAMES TROUP, QUOTED IN THE VICTORIA *Colonist*, NOVEMBER 1923.

The *Princess Kathleen*, at left and below, is nearly ready to leave the John Brown yards at Clydebank for the Pacific Coast. –DR. W. B. CHUNG COLLECTION

The Ultimate Princesses

DESPITE THE SUCCESS OF THE *Princess Louise* built in North Vancouver, when replacements for the *Margaret* and *Irene* were ordered, the CPR returned to the Clyde and the famous John Brown shipyards for the new steamships. Troup explained that, "the class of machinery that will go into these vessels cannot be built anywhere in this country. It will be of a grade much higher than anything we have now; and it is not practicable to build the hulls here and the engines elsewhere for ships such as we have in mind."[26] Capt. Troup travelled to Great Britain to place the orders for two new steamers in November 1923. John Brown & Company's bid was for £223,000 per vessel with delivery promised in 11 months. Outfitting the steamers with linens, embroidered quilts, crockery, glassware, silverplate, mattresses, pillows, library books, barber and manicurist shops, chronometers, a Sperry Gyro Compass, and furnishings cost an additional £19,224 for each steamer. The total included £294 to purchase a Steinway grand piano for the shelter deck's social hall, writing room and sitting room, which had a dance floor, and £54 for a smaller Cramer piano for the observation room on the promenade deck.

The vessels were to be impressive: 5908 gross tons, 368 feet, 9 inches (112.4 m) in overall length, a breadth of 60 feet (18.3 m), daytime certificates for 1800 passengers, seats for 159 in the dining rooms, 153 staterooms providing 309 beds and berths, a crew of 148 and compound turbine engines, developing 17,000 horsepower, driving twin screws for a maximum speed of 22.5 knots (nearly 26 miles or 42 km an hour). But these statistics were only the skeletal outline. The design was striking and elegant and the vessels' interiors were completed with an attention to detail and design that was extraordinary. Troup and his staff, as well as CPR's officials in Britain, devoted many hours to making the vessels first-class throughout. As Troup had stated many years before with the construction of the *Princess Victoria*, it was the details that "go to make up the whole affair." In nearly 25 years, his approach to the fitting out of his ships had changed very little.

By early October, 1924, 1,500 men were at work on the two *Princesses* with joinery work progressing, the boilers installed and the turbines being fitted. These vessels, to be named the *Princess Marguerite* and *Princess Kathleen*, were destined to become the finest coastal liners to join the fleet since the construction of the *Victoria* and the *Charlotte* 20 years before. They were the zenith of Capt. Troup's accomplishments in ship design and became famous for their fast and luxurious service on the Triangle Route.

The *Kathleen* was launched on September 27, 1924 and christened by Lady Mount Stephen and the *Marguerite* followed on November 29, 1924, christened by Marguerite

Kathleen Shaughnessy for whom the new steamer was named. Completed early in January 1925, the *Kathleen* sailed for Victoria on January 15, 1925. Nearly a month later, the *Princess Louise*, with 1000 people on board, greeted the *Kathleen* off William Head and followed her into Victoria's Inner Harbour at 3:15 on Friday afternoon, February 13, 1925. Crowds lined the streets around the harbour in greeting. The two *Princesses* brought nothing but accolades for the CPR, the Coast Service and Capt. Troup, who was honoured at a dinner hosted by Victoria's Mayor J. C. Pendray on February 16, 1925. Speakers included Premier John Oliver. A month later, Mrs. Troup and Mrs. Neroutsos, wife of Assistant Manager Capt. Cyril Neroutsos, hosted an "at home" on the *Princess Kathleen*.

On March 25, 1925, the *Marguerite* sailed from the John Brown yards and began the 9,000-mile (14 500-km) journey to Victoria which she completed at 5:00 p.m. on April 20. Unfortunately, Second Officer C. Hawick who had been sent to hospital in Colon, Panama, had died of typhoid on the 19th.

The *Kathleen* entered service in May after a drydocking and final inspection in Victoria. Capt. James Boyce must have been a proud man as he looked down from the bridge of his fine new ship. A veteran of 25 years with the CPR, he began with the company as an able seaman and had advanced to be captain on several *Princesses* including the *Victoria* and the *Charlotte* on the Triangle Run. The first few days were devoted to special preview and trial trips with several hundred invited guests aboard from each of the Triangle Route terminal cities. On the 12th, the *Kathleen* ran full speed from Victoria to Seattle. "I think we should take a fairly good trial out of her going up to fully 200 revolutions any way," wrote James McGowan, superintendent engineer to W.E. Oliver, the *Kathleen*'s Chief Engineer. McGowan was not to be disappointed when soon after, the *Kathleen* cleared Brotchie Ledge just past Ogden Point, and "the throb of the engines grew to a muffled roar," reported the *Colonist*, and "the *Kathleen* responded instantly, leaping forward like a greyhound unleashed." The overall time from Brotchie Ledge to the Bell Street terminal in Seattle was just 2 hours and 55 minutes, for a speed of 23.3 knots (26.8 miles or 43 km an hour). "She has done as we expected," commented Capt. Troup, in classic understatement, for the *Vancouver Sun*.

The next day she ran back to Victoria, and on the 14th made another trip to Seattle and then steamed overnight to Vancouver for a layover day before taking an excursion to Jervis Inlet. The next day, May 17, 1925, the *Princess Kathleen* and the *Princess Marguerite* started officially on the Triangle Run.

The two new steamers were a resounding success and the public responded with great enthusiasm. Early in August, Troup wired to CPR Vice-President D. C. Coleman that "the two new steamers on the Triangle have made wonderful showing in gross earnings for July.

Bon voyage...

"To you and your officers greetings and bon voyage and my sincerest good wishes for the success and prosperity of the *Princess Kathleen* which I was so proud to launch."

—GIANA MOUNT STEPHEN. (MARCONIGRAM TO CAPT. TROUP, JANUARY 19, 1925, FROM LONDON).

Love at first sight...

"My first encounter with the *Kathleen* came one Friday in February 1925 when she sailed into Victoria Harbour for the first time. After school that day a friend and I swarmed over that ship from stem to stern—from bridge to engine room."

"The finest B.C. Coast vessels of all time. Speedy, handsome, with beautiful woodwork in their public rooms. They ruled the Triangle run—sometimes seasonally—sometimes all year—from 1925 until their sad departure for war service in the autumn of '41. *Marguerite* never came back."

—TOM GOODLAKE, BCCSS PURSER.

Capt. Troup with Commissioner George Lamping of the Port of Seattle and Capt. James Boyce on the *Princess Kathleen* on her first trip to Seattle. —EARL J. MARSH COLLECTION

Luxury afloat...

"Everything dear to the heart of luxury-loving women is represented in the beautiful ship which has recently arrived.... Seated in the spacious dining saloon sipping tea and nibbling delicious cakes to the strains of the *Princess Kathleen* orchestra, one had a foretaste of the luxurious pleasure of travelling on the vessel as a passenger when the boat is put into regular service."

–*Daily Colonist*, MARCH 28, 1925.

Much in excess of any previous showing [for the] B.C. Coast Service." At the end of their first summer they had carried 267,000 passengers. The gamble on the new vessels was paying off and Coast Service officials were relieved; they were all too aware that all of the investment in fine machinery and accommodations had to be recovered and a profit made in a short summer season of peak travel.

The beautiful steamship was photographed by Clinton Betz at Seattle on a chilly grey day in October 1940. To maintain the double service on the Triangle Route the *Kathleen* was based in Victoria and the *Marguerite* in Vancouver. In later years, as the service expanded, the *Princess Joan* normally ran out of Vancouver and the *Elizabeth* from Victoria. –CLINTON BETZ

The Victoria, the Kathleen and Capt. Troup...

"On Wednesday morning, the *Princess Victoria* left Seattle for Victoria at 9:00 a.m. This is the run which the *Victoria* has served with phenomenal regularity for nearly a quarter of a century. Still one of the fastest merchant ships afloat, the *Victoria* has no reason to bow her head in any company, but in speed and appointments she is surpassed by her young sister, the *Kathleen*. The latter left Seattle at 10:00 a.m., and, unhampered by a schedule, could have beaten the *Victoria* to the terminal in James Bay [Victoria]. About noon the *Kathleen* perceptibly slackened speed. An executive officer of the Canadian Pacific on board noticed this and, surmising the reason, said to the Manager [Capt. James Troup] of the Coast Service, 'I observe your strategy. You did not wish us to humiliate the old flagship of the fleet.' And the answer was perfectly frank: 'You're right. The *Victoria* has been a wonder, she has been the backbone of the fleet for years, and she must not give way to any newcomer in the family.'

"And so the *Princess Victoria*, unmolested and unchallenged, swept into the harbour at Victoria at 1:15, sharp on time, as she has done for so many years."

—FROM AN UNSIGNED LETTER FORWARDED TO GRANT HALL, VICE-PRESIDENT, MONTREAL, MAY 13, 1925.

A Special Treat...

"Don's folks took us over when Donna, our daughter, was small and we had a meal in the dining room and it was beautiful. White cloths, silver and the service was excellent. Donna just couldn't believe it. It was heaven to her and it was to us too. It was beautiful; that was the *Kathleen*." –PHYLLIS HORNE

"Workmen were still reconditioning her, working on her after the war. The waiters were so nice and so good to the kids. It was truly beautiful." –DON HORNE

-PHYLLIS AND DON HORNE RECALLING FAMILY TRAVELS ON THE *Kathleen* IN THE 1940S.

The *Marguerite*, above, on April 5, 1939 and the *Kathleen*, at left, on September 8, 1931, entering Vancouver Harbour. –LORNE CAMPBELL COLLECTION; MAURICE CHANDLER, AUTHOR'S COLLECTION

Twin Screw Turbine Steamers
Princess Kathleen and Princess Marguerite

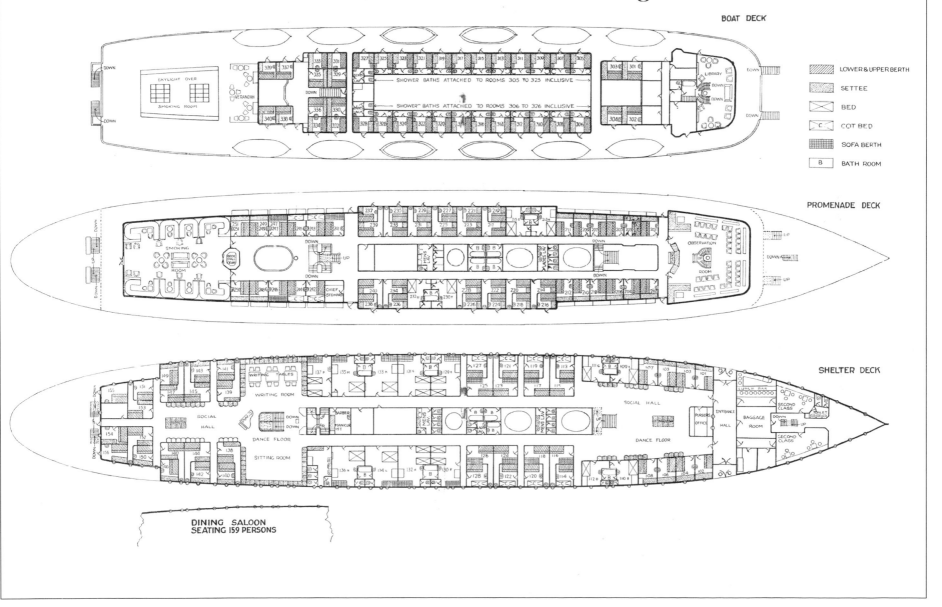

Deck plans of the *Kathleen* and *Marguerite* from the CPR's 1925 Triangle Route booklet. –Dr. W. B. Chung collection

The magnificent, new and specially appointed *Princess Steamships* that operate on the triangle service between Victoria, Vancouver and Seattle are the last word in marine accommodation. These palatial twin screw steamships leave daily throughout the year in each direction.

Dinner

Hors d'Œuvres Varies

Oyster Cocktail

Cheese Straws   Ripe Olives   Celery en Branche

Puree of Asparagus   Consomme Royale

Steamed Salmon, Cucumber Sauce Brevette

Crimped Halibut, Potatoes Parisienne

Calves' Head a la Poulette   Cumberland Ham, Fried Sweet Potatoes

Golden Buck   Pineapple Fritter, Custard Sauce

TO ORDER, 10 MINUTES: "Marguerite" Mixed Grill

Prime Ribs Beef, Yorkshire Pudding

Roast Island Turkey, Cranberry Jelly

Stuffed Tomatoes   Demidoff Salad

Mashed and Brown Potatoes   Macedoine of Vegetables

Apple Pie   Boston Pudding, Maple Sauce   Strawberry Tartlets

French Pancake   Compote of Peaches

Princess Ice Cream

MacLaren's Imperial, Roquefort and Stilton Cheese

Fresh Fruit   Walnuts   Assorted Cake

Demi Tasse

The Dinner menu from the *Princess Kathleen* and *Princess Marguerite* for 1925 featured a typical selection of CPR cuisine. –AUTHOR'S COLLECTION

Dining on the Kathleen...

"The *Kathleen* was a truly beautiful ship, and I have had other people tell me that after her post-war refit and her entry into the Alaska cruise service, her interior was even better that it was when she was new. She was beautifully maintained. The food in the dining room was better than on the CNR and there was plenty of it. It was typical CPR food, but served with a flare. I learned early in the voyage to eat the things that they do best, you know, roast beef and other dishes. They had marvellous plum pudding, which I had every time I'd go. Marvellous soups."

–COMMODORE LESTER G. ARELLANES, 1990.

For a Young Man, a Briefing was in Order...

"That was a 'first class' experience. When we travelled, I was always required to wear a coat and tie (unlike people and kids who travel today). I was always given a little briefing by my father or mother before we went to the dining room about using the various knives, forks and spoons, as the dining room provided a full silver service. Dining aboard the *Marguerite* and *Kathleen* was truly an elegant experience. My father was a 'meat and potatoes' type of person, but he would usually order poached salmon, new potatoes with parsley and green peas for his entree if it was available We always started with soup. My mother always enjoyed either a crab or oyster cocktail after soup. Dessert, for me, was orange sherbet and my father usually opted for cheese. I think that the CPR ships accounted for my first introduction to finger bowls. A quaint custom rarely seen anymore even in five star hotels."

–KEN KNOX, 1998, RECALLING THE *Princesses* ON THE TRIANGLE ROUTE BEFORE THE SECOND WORLD WAR.

The dining room, at right, was one of the key features of a vessel's passenger accommodations and the 159-seat saloons on the *Kathleen* and *Marguerite* were beautifully appointed. Later as many as 175 people could be accommodated. The saloon extended across the full width of the ship and was decorated in a Louis XVI style and was panelled in tones of ivory, with doors and other fittings in mahogany. Paired oval windows in the ship's sides gave light and were curtained in rich red silk. Flooring was a green and white tile. Tables were arranged for parties of 6, 8 and 14.[27] –BEDFORD LEMERE photo, DR. W. B. CHUNG collection

Fine interior decor...

"The 'deluxe' staterooms probably provoked most admiration, the color motif in each room tracing its way through the upholstering of the furniture, the heavy silk tapestry hangings round the beds, the candle shades and other details. One room, finished in mahogany, was decorated throughout in rose and olive green; another, finished in satinwood, had hangings of a rich plum shade, another in Pekin blue and gold. Twin beds, each completely screened with long silk hangings, are found in several of these suites and all suites have their individual bathrooms, big dressing tables, and long mirrors."

–*Daily Colonist*, March 28, 1925.

One of the *Kathleen's* deluxe staterooms, at left, the library, below, the spacious forward observation room on the promenade deck, above right, and the forward social hall and staircase. –Bedford Lemere photos, Dr. W. B. Chung collection

The Kathleen's Smoking Lounge...

Troup devoted many hours to the design of the smoking lounge on after end of the promenade deck. His plan was to incorporate what he described as British Columbia Coast art and to this end he consulted the architect Francis M. Rattenbury for design suggestions and corresponded with Harlan Smith, Archaeologist at the Victoria Memorial Museum (a predecessor of the Canadian Museum of Civilization) in Ottawa. To Smith he wrote, "I am quite in accord with your views that we should do all we can to keep North American Indian art from going completely out of existence, and out of memory." He also consulted with C. F. Newcombe at the British Columbia Provincial Museum (much later the Royal British Columbia Museum) in Victoria. "Rattenbury proposes to make the capitals of the columns with four extending prows of Indian canoes," wrote Troup to J. H. Alexander, the CPR's inspector at the John Brown yards in April 1924, "and he proposes to work up some absolutely Indian designs for panels and conventional totem pole pilasters, which can be used elsewhere." The designs prepared by Troup and Rattenbury apparently were not fully adopted because work had already started but the panel and totem suggestions were included. The work was "given out to a firm in the south of England." Six totem carvings were done in Black Bean wood, a very different material from the traditional Western Redcedar used on the Northwest Coast, and the centre poles were "crowned with a reproduction of the Waw-Waw Indian Mythological Bird" (presumably referring to a Thunderbird). Two large skylights featured "brilliantly coloured leaded glass."[28] There is no suggestion that anyone considered consulting or contracting with First Nations artists to do the work.

The elaborately decorated smoking room, above, on the *Kathleen*. At left, the *Marguerite*, backing away into Burrard Inlet before steaming past Stanley Park on the way to Victoria and Seattle. On the facing page, the 1925 Triangle service brochure and timetable. —BEDFORD LEMERE PHOTO, DR. W. B. CHUNG COLLECTION; CANADIAN PACIFIC ARCHIVES; DR. W. B. CHUNG COLLECTION; VANCOUVER MARITIME MUSEUM

THE TRIANGLE SERVICE

VANCOUVER

VICTORIA

SEATTLE

PRINCESS KATHLEEN

PRINCESS MARGUERITE

EMPRESS HOTEL, VICTORIA.

SEATTLE

VANCOUVER HOTEL

CANADIAN PACIFIC B.C. COAST S.S. SERVICE

Seattle Piers...

In 1922 the BCCSS moved its wharf offices and facilities in Seattle from Pier 1 to the Coleman Dock at the foot of Marion Street to provide better access and improved facilities for passengers. In 1925 the service shifted to the Bell Street Dock. Then in 1930 a more elaborate and modern terminal was opened at the Lenora Street Pier, which the *Port of Seattle Bulletin* described as being "within easy access to the business and hotel district, [and] well adapted for passenger and freight business."[29] Finally in December 1976 the *Marguerite* moved to Pier 69.

Canadian Pacific Railway Company
STEAMSHIP LINES

British Columbia Coast Steamship Service

VANCOUVER - VICTORIA - SEATTLE

Luxurious
New Turbine
Steamships

Princess Kathleen

and

Princess Marguerite

THE TRIANGLE ROUTE

EFFECTIVE SEPTEMBER 14, 1925
DAILY SERVICE

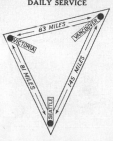

VANCOUVER-SEATTLE via Victoria	
Lv. Vancouver	10.30 a.m.
Ar. Victoria	3.00 p.m.
Lv. Victoria	4.30 p.m.
Ar. Seattle	9.00 p.m.

SEATTLE-VANCOUVER via Victoria	
Lv. Seattle	9.00 a.m.
Ar. Victoria	1.15 p.m.
Lv. Victoria	2.15 p.m.
Ar. Vancouver	7.00 p.m.

VANCOUVER-SEATTLE Direct	
Lv. Vancouver	11.00 p.m.
Ar. Seattle	8.00 a.m.

SEATTLE-VANCOUVER Direct	
Lv. Seattle	11.30 p.m.
Ar. Vancouver	8.00 a.m.

VANCOUVER - VICTORIA

DAILY SERVICE

Lv. Vancouver	11.45 p.m.	Lv. Victoria	11.45 p.m.
Ar. Victoria	7.00 a.m.	Ar. Vancouver	7.00 a.m.

Schedule subject to weather and tidal conditions and to change without notice.

TICKET OFFICES	Vancouver, B.C.	Victoria, B.C.	Seattle, Wash.
	W. S. STEWART, Hotel Vancouver Agent	H. S. HOWARD, Wharf Agent	A. M. ANDERSON, Coleman Dock Agent
	S. G. LEMMON, Wharf Agent	L. D. CHETHAM,	J. T. HAGGIN, City Ticket Agent
	C. MILLARD, Depot Ticket Agent	District Passenger Agent	E. L. SHEEHAN, General Agent
	F. H. DALY, City Passenger Agent	1102 Government St.	608 Second Avenue
	434 Hastings Street West		

C. H. BOWES
Asst. General Passenger Agent
VANCOUVER, B.C.

W. H. SNELL
General Passenger Agent
VANCOUVER, B.C.

J. W. TROUP
Mgr. B. C. C. S.
Victoria, B. C.

PRINTED IN CANADA

For Nanaimo, the Princess Elaine

WITH THE *Kathleen* AND *Marguerite* WELL IN HAND and a buoyant economy, Troup and his staff turned their attention to the rest of the fleet, which was being strained to meet traffic demands. Several areas in particular needed attention and new vessels. The automobile ferry service and the Vancouver–Nanaimo route was the first to be addressed. The *Princess Patricia* was already 25 years old and had very limited capacity for vehicles. In fact, vehicle accommodations were so restricted, with a clearance of just six feet (1.8 m), that she could only handle automobiles whose tops could be lowered or very small hard-top cars. Sometimes it was even necessary to let the air out of a car's tires to squeeze it on board. Nonetheless, the *Patricia* operated profitably and the *Charmer* or *Motor Princess* were used in the summer to carry additional vehicle traffic. Capt. Troup, being concerned about the high costs of a new vessel, considered rebuilding the *Princess Victoria*, whose engines and boilers, he felt, should last a further 10 years as an automobile ferry. However, as early as October 1924, Troup received preliminary quotations from John Brown & Company at Clydebank, Scotland, for a new steamer and by 1925 the business community at Nanaimo was lobbying hard for an improved automobile ferry service; by that December, Troup was developing plans for an 18-knot (21-mile or 33-km an hour) intercity ferry that could carry about 40 automobiles and have a passenger capacity of 1200. Troup considered the development of new ferry slips that would permit bow and stern loading of a ferry but decided against it because of the high costs of terminal development and instead recommended a traditional side-loading vessel.[30] The planning progressed by the autumn of 1926 into the three-funnelled, triple-screw, geared-turbine-powered *Princess Elaine*, built by John Brown & Company. She was launched on October 26, 1927 and left the Clyde for Vancouver on March 17, 1928, under the command of Capt. R. N. Stuart, VC, for the long voyage to Victoria where she arrived without incident on April 25 to a welcoming reception.

To facilitate vehicle loading, a turntable was installed on the Main Deck of the *Elaine* to help manoeuvre automobiles around the limited deck space, but the system was slow, inconvenient and cumbersome. It was a conservative decision that was a step backward from the developments evident in the *Motor Princess*. Although in many ways a modern vessel that made a dramatic improvement to the service, the *Princess Elaine* was still essentially a conservative design and it did not place the CPR in the forefront of handling automobile traffic on the Pacific Coast.

Decisions on design and specifications were not entirely in Troup's hands and he had some disagreements with management over the new steamer but in the end all involved

The Princess Patricia was profitable....

"The *Princess Patricia* has been very successful and has made her cost many times over... her net profits have been $775,194.38, while her cost to us in 1912 was just about $180,000, so that if we leave, say, $100,000.00 distributed through the years, for extraordinary expenditures and renewals..., we would still have a fair margin of profit. The *Patricia* is now 22 years old and the up-keep on her is increasing all the time. Her propellers are small and near the surface, and are continually getting into trouble with logs, so that I feel it is time we were considering a replacement."

–CAPT. TROUP TO D.C. COLEMAN, VICE-PRESIDENT, APRIL 29, 1924.

Pride in the Princess Elaine...

"You know my personal pride in completing a vessel exactly to Contract without extras, and I am delighted that this has been accomplished in the *Princess Elaine*,... Knowing your critical eye and your high standard, I cannot hope that the *Elaine* will escape without some criticism, but I do really think that she should prove a valuable and successful addition to your fine fleet."

–SIR THOMAS BELL, JOHN BROWN & COMPANY, TO CAPT. TROUP, MARCH 3, 1928.

The *Princess Elaine*, shown at right on one of her first voyages from Vancouver to Nanaimo, was a familiar sight in Vancouver. Below is her coffee shop.
–CYRIL LITTLEBURY, AUTHOR'S COLLECTION; LORNE CAMPBELL COLLECTION

seem to have been pleased with the *Elaine*. She performed very well on trials and could handle the Vancouver-Nanaimo service easily in 2 hours and 15 minutes if necessary. Troup had also argued for the rebuilding of the *Princess Victoria* as an automobile ferry, convinced that this would be a cheaper alternative, but management apparently preferred new construction. Moreover, Troup hoped for a single-screw design for reasons of economy but in the end settled for the more expensive and complex triple-screw propulsion system to obtain the speed desired for the service.

An interesting footnote to the *Elaine's* design was that her passenger deck was built to allow for the installation of staterooms for overnight service, making the steamer potentially suitable for either the Triangle Route or Alaskan service but these modifications were never made. The *Elaine* is seldom remembered with the same affection as some of the other *Princesses* because she was a day boat without many of the amenities of the Triangle Route steamers. Functional, and relatively plain, without the design elegance of her running mates, "she could not be termed a luxury ship," recalled Tom Goodlake who was her purser in 1930. She had "rows of none-too-comfortable long benches [and] a coffee shop with one waitress."[31] When new she was a smooth-running steamer but veteran patrons recall in her later years the clattering of dishes and the dancing of coffee mugs on the tables as she reversed engines and gathered speed leaving harbour. Perhaps the vibration was a symptom of having hit too many logs and deadheads over the years on her thousands of trips back and forth between Vancouver and Nanaimo or Victoria.

The *Elaine's* first year was trouble-plagued although in ways that were unrelated to her service on the Vancouver-Nanaimo route. After some introductory cruises and before entering regular service, she was pulled out for inspection at the Victoria Machinery Depot's marine ways in Victoria's Inner Harbour but the hauling gear broke and one man was killed and two were seriously injured. Despite the tragedy, the new steamer was in service on May 7th and proved popular and successful. However, she was pulled out again in September for routine docking. All went well until she was to be refloated, when the cradle stuck, stranding the steamer and there she remained from early September until December 15, 1928, when, after extensive preliminary work, she was pulled back into the water by the tug *Salvage King*. The *Elaine's* delayed re-entry into service made it necessary to use the *Princess Pat* and the *Charmer* on the Nanimo route that fall.[32] After that, Tom Goodlake recalled, "they used the Esquimalt drydock for overhauls [and] she worked faithfully on the Nanaimo run for 23 years, when displaced in 1951 by the *Princess of Nanaimo*."

The Coast Service was always having to juggle the operation of its vessels to provide the most efficient use of its steamers for the traffic and also to cover refits and accidents. The

The *Elaine* stuck high and dry on the marine railway at the Victoria Machinery Depot's shipyard in Victoria in 1928. –B.C. ARCHIVES, HP16886

Thousands of people travelled on the *Elaine* between Vancouver and Nanaimo, to the Gulf Islands and to Victoria in her long career. As a young man, photographer Albert H. Paull recorded these scenes, including the Nanaimo wharf, in 1928 when the steamer was a new and exciting addition to the coastal fleet. Facilities at Nanaimo were improved significantly after the Second World War to handle the growing automobile traffic and to accommodate the new *Princess of Nanaimo*. –AUTHOR'S COLLECTION

arrival of a new vessel such as the *Princess Elaine,* or the retirement of an elderly ship, usually had a ripple effect on the assignment of vessels. The much larger automobile capacity on the *Elaine* made possible the reassignment of the *Motor Princess* and the *Charmer,* by then in its waning years, as well as freeing the old *Princess Pat* for less demanding but lucrative work as an excursion steamer. The next year a new summer-only, double daily automobile ferry service began between Steveston, south of Vancouver, and Sidney, on Vancouver Island, using the *Motor Princess.* The concept was to provide a short ferry crossing, particularly appealing to motorists. As well, Steveston could be reached by British Columbia Electric Railway interurban trains from Vancouver. The *Charmer,* with over 40 years of steaming the coast behind her, was used as a relief steamer and was to end her career at Newcastle Island, near Nanaimo, as an accommodations vessel. The *Princess Pat* proved a tough old vessel. Because no replacement was available in the mid-1920s, her stern and one turbine had been rebuilt and overall she was still in good condition. Beginning in 1930 with the sale of the little *Island Princess,* she provided a weekend summer service to the Gulf Islands from Victoria and Vancouver complementing the more frequent sailings of the *Princess Royal* which had relieved the little steamer *Otter* which was retired. However, these services proved to be only a temporary adjustment and with declining traffic in the Depression years, the layup of the older and less efficient vessels and the eventual and inevitable retirement of both the *Pat* and the *Royal* in the mid-1930s. The *Princess Mary* became the mainstay of the Gulf Islands service while at the same time covering the Powell River route.

Capt. James W. Troup

JAMES WILLIAM TROUP WAS BORN IN PORTLAND, OREGON, on February 5, 1855 to a seafaring family. His grandfather, Capt. James Turnbull, ran a steamer between Portland and Vancouver and his father, Capt. W. H. Troup, born in England, was an experienced steamboat captain on the Lower Columbia. At age 12 Troup was already working on the boats with his father and grandfather steering the steamers on the Lower Columbia. "He was so short," recalled Earl Marsh, "they had to put an apple box for him to stand on behind the wheel." By the age of 20 he was master of the steamer *Wasp*. By the 1880s he was working in British Columbia as master of the Fraser River steamer *William Irving* and the big old sidewheeler *Yosemite* that would one day be part of the fleet he would manage. He also worked on the Thompson River boats. He returned to Washington and Oregon and then came back to B.C. in the 1890s to manage the steamers of the Columbia & Kootenay Steam Navigation Company in the Kootenay district. There his forte for steamer design was really unleashed and he created a generation of lake and river steamers that were the backbone of the inland fleet. In 1897-98 he came to the coast to build sternwheelers for the CPR's unsuccessful Stikine River service and then returned to Nelson, where he was superintendent. Then, in 1901, he came to the coast to manage the new British Columbia Coast Service and he had truly found his calling. But he also continued his long relationship with the Interior vessels and worked on the design of the next generations of sternwheelers for the Kootenay and Okanagan districts.

From an early age, Troup showed a flair for steamboat design and he proved very good at it. With very little formal education, he had almost an intuitive understanding of the elements of hull design, engine performance and the subtleties of construction that distinguished an outstanding ship.

Troup married Frances Julia Stump, of Sacramento, California, in 1879 and they had a son, Roy Wayne, and a daughter Winona. After moving to Victoria, Troup commissioned architect Samuel McClure to design a large house called *Tidaldean* overlooking Victoria harbour in 1905. It was built at a cost of $10,000. Roy Wayne Troup became a steamboat captain operating vessels in many parts of British Columbia and Winona married a prominent doctor, Harold M. Eberts. Troup was an early automobile enthusiast having the second license issued in British Columbia and was president of the Victoria Automobile Club. The Troups were well-connected in business and social circles and entertained the rich and the famous at their home.

One Coast Service oldtimer related how Troup, would drive to his home for lunch and, legend has it, sit at the table with his watch beside him. He would listen for the whistle of any ships coming in or sailing from Victoria and if they were late, the tardy captain would be reminded of the importance of schedule keeping when Troup returned to the office that afternoon. Troup was a complex man, capable, talented, demanding, a perfectionist; sometimes called an autocrat. A man of great personal experience, he could be a difficult master. "He was a pretty tough man, but

Capt. James W. Troup and Capt. Douglas Brown during the height of Troup's career as manager of the British Columbia Coast Steamship Service. –EARL J. MARSH COLLECTION

The *Princess Marguerite* and *Princess Kathleen*, shown at right passing off Victoria's Ogden Point, were the culmination of Troup's career as a designer of fine coastal liners. –GOWARD SUTTON PHOTO, RBCM, 972.263.69ba

Capt. Troup, seated at left, poses with officials and guests. This photo was most likely taken on the inaugural voyage of the *Princess Kathleen* in 1925. Seated beside Troup is Canadian Pacific's Vice-President Grant Hall and standing at far right is Capt. Cyril Neroutsos, who was to succeed Troup as manager of the Coast Service. Behind Grant Hall is Capt. Robert W. McMurray who became manager in 1934. —CARL F. TIMMS, VANCOUVER MARITIME MUSEUM

he was perceptive. Some of them hated him," commented Earl Marsh. "He was a quiet man. I didn't get very close to him," recalled Earl who in the early days of his long Coast Service career was an office boy and later an assistant accountant in the offices before Troup retired. "The only time I really talked to him was when he retired [on September 1, 1928]. He asked each of us in and talked to us with tears rolling down his cheeks. He was 73. Ships were his whole life."

The CPR honoured Troup with a retirement dinner on the *Princess Louise* on September 15, 1928. General Superintendent C. A. Cotterell lauded Troup for the fleet that he described as the finest of its kind in the world and a monument to Troup. In toasting Troup, Capt. Neroutsos praised his old boss: "In 27 years Capt. Troup has never broken his word to man or officer."[33]

Troup was tired, his health was suffering from the stress of office and its heavy responsibility, undoubtedly amplified by his own determination to do things his own way, and his advancing years. On August 24, 1928, he wrote to Dr. Charles S. Douglas, consulting naval architect, Glasgow, who was assisting with the *Princess Norah*, then under construction. "I regret, in a way," he said, "I did not remain to see this little ship completed and in service, but I was anxious to be relieved, and to have my leisure before it comes too late, hence my retirement." He seemed ready for retirement but he was still consulted by Neroutsos and the CPR officials on details of Coast Service management and his opinion was sought frequently on the new steamers being built in Scotland. Canadian Pacific continued to pay Troup his full salary throughout his retirement years.

Capt. James Troup died at the age of 76 from bronchitis and heart disease on November 30, 1931, just three years after his retirement. At 2:30 p.m., on December 2, 1931, the time of his funeral in Victoria's Christ Church Cathedral, the *Princesses*, all along the Coast, stopped for two minutes in tribute to the man who had contributed so much to the Coast Service. His *Princess Kathleen*, en route to Vancouver, hove-to off Ross Bay cemetery and dipped her flags in tribute.

The Princess Norah, the "Good Ship Maquinna," & the way of the coast

THE *Elaine* WAS FOLLOWED TO THE COAST by the *Princess Norah*, a somewhat larger and improved version of the ill-fated *Princess Sophia*. Built by the Fairfield yards at Govan, Scotland, she was a sturdy vessel intended for the Vancouver Island West Coast and the North Coast routes. She featured a large cargo capacity as well as 62 staterooms and was licensed with a day certificate of 450 passengers. The *Norah*, with a triple-expansion engine and single screw, was fitted with a rudder in the bow to make manoeuvring in the restricted waters of the coastal inlets easier and safer. One large funnel and two masts gave the stocky, 262-foot (79.8-m) vessel a sturdy and business-like appearance. Several firms submitted bids for building the steamer including Burrard Dry Dock in North Vancouver, but Burrard's estimate of $860,000 was well above Fairfield's offer of £112,000 even allowing for the additional cost of delivering the vessel from the Clyde.[34]

The *Norah* was launched on September 27, 1928, and on November 14 she completed her trials reaching a maximum speed of just over 15 knots (17.25 miles or 27.8 km an hour) at 140 revolutions.[35] Difficulties arose from the overheating of the main bearings, which took some time to rectify. After repairs and modifications were made, she was accepted by the CPR on December 20, 1928, and sailed later that day for Victoria. Once on the Pacific Coast, the *Norah* became a welcome addition to the fleet and usually sailed on the West Coast of Vancouver Island route during the summer months and to Alaska and North Coast ports each winter.

Even with the arrival of the *Norah*, the Vancouver Island West Coast service still really belonged to the *Maquinna*. Over a 40-year career she strayed little from the three-times-a-month service from Victoria northward along the rugged and stormy coast to settlements as distant as Port Alice near the northern end of Vancouver Island. Storms, delays in port, tides and fog could delay her passage up and down the coast and each night Vancouver's *Daily Province* sponsored a radio newscast and Earle Kelly, the announcer, told people all along her route just where the *Maquinna* was at 4:00 that afternoon. They could judge just when they needed to meet the *Maquinna* on her rounds. "The *Daily Province*," noted the newspaper on December 23, 1936, "through its news announcer, wishes Capt. Ernie Thomson, his officers and crew, and the people his good ship serves, a Happy Christmas and a Prosperous New Year." On such traditions legends grow but the place of the *Maquinna* in the history of the West Coast already was secure.

The Princess Norah was designed for the Pacific...
"One important feature of this ship which must not be overlooked is that she is to operate in the open sea, and must have full classification, and full scantlings, not any compromise measure like the Seattle-Skagway, or other limited certificate. This boat will be used in an entirely different trade to the *Princess Adelaide* and *Princess Charlotte*. ...with the *Princess Maquinna* as a guide, you can form a better idea perhaps, of the requirements."
—CAPT. TROUP TO FAIRFIELD SHIPBUILDING & ENGINEERING CO., DECEMBER 30, 1927.

The *Princess Norah,* at right, was a classic passenger and freight steamer designed for the British Columbia and Alaska coastal trade. –JOHN NEWMAN

Cargo from isolated ports on the West Coast of Vancouver Island and on the coastal routes between Vancouver and Alaska was a key to the financial success of the Coast Steamship Service. The great tidal fluctuations along the coast, clear in this photo as the *Norah* almost disappears below the wharf, show why, in part, the CPR steamers were designed with nearly vertical sides above the main deck. –RICHARD SPURWAY, AUTHOR'S COLLECTION

West Coast Route dilemma...

"I think it was at Tofino that we realized to our absolute horror that we were running out of Scotch. The only licensed premises were at Port Alberni. So I asked the Purser first. 'Where do you think we could get another bottle of Scotch?' And he said, 'Not 'til we get back to Port Alberni. It's the only licensed premises.' Oh, God! So then I told this man, a commercial traveller, what the situation was. 'Don't worry about that. We can get a bottle.' At Tofino, he zipped up to make his calls, and came back with not one, but two bottles! We finally ran out of that, and I think we replenished our supply again either at Ucluelet or Port Alberni, but there was no more worry about waiting for licensed premises, because it was available every place that you stopped if you knew the right people."

–Commodore Lester G. Arellanes, 1990, deliberating on the vicissitudes and tribulations of West Coast travel on the *Maquinna*.

The new *Princess Norah* was intended to relieve the aging *Maquinna* and expand the services available but with the coming of the Great Depression of the 1930s and the Second World War it was the *Maquinna* that continued on the West Coast route far more than her younger running mate, which was most often assigned to the North Coastal services. The *Norah* worked on the West Coast of Vancouver Island during the summers, with the *Maquinna* often running a complementary schedule, but each winter the *Norah* went back on the Alaska and North Coast routes, leaving the open stormy Pacific to the little *Maquinna*.

The *Maquinna's* logs recorded many memorable incidents but unusual events, memorable as they were, present an incomplete portrait. The essence of the story of the *Maquinna* lies elsewhere in the day-to-day service the old steamer provided to countless people all along that rugged and dangerous coast. They depended on the *Maquinna* for mail, packages, groceries, news, cargo, supplies and for visits from friends, doctors and family. They were seldom disappointed by the *Maquinna* or her dedicated officers and crew who felt a personal responsibility to the people of the coast. Her captains included Edward Gillam, who was a Justice of the Peace and able to deal with legal matters in the little ports, Reg. "Red" Thomson, William "Black" Thomson, P.L. Leslie, Leonard W. McDonald, Martin MacKinnon and Ralph A. Carthew, seasoned men who knew the ways of the coast all too well.

"Friends are permitted to roam through the ship's innards at will until five minutes before sailing time," recalled George Nicholson, West Coast author. "Warning whistles are blown at all stopping places, giving those sightseeing ashore ample time to return to the ship. Afternoon tea and midnight supper is served to all through passengers. A stewardess takes care of the women and children. The senior officers dine with the passengers, the captain at his table and the chief officer, chief engineer, and purser at the other tables in the saloon.... Bridge, music and dancing is enjoyed in the evenings and often the ship's officers and passengers all take in a dance ashore at some remote cannery or logging camp."[36]

Navigating the rugged coast of Vancouver Island left its share of scares on the tough little *Princess Maquinna*. In February 1919, she lost her propeller at Easy Cove in Kyuquot Sound; in September 1922 she grounded on a rocky ledge in Esperanza Inlet; in July 1927, she hit a rock off Hecate Wharf in Esperanza Inlet and three years later she grounded at Matilda Creek in Clayoquot Sound; in 1934 she collided with the steamer *Masunda* near Port Alberni and in 1949 she ran over the gas boat *Lorraine* with a loss of three lives, and there were other memorable adventures including hitting Ripple Rock in Seymour Narrows. She also carried the Marquis of Willingdon, the Governor-General of Canada, and other dignitaries in 1924 and tried vainly to rescue the crew of the *Carelmapu* in 1915.[37]

Individual recollections of the *Maquinna* told of dense fogs with the old steamer easing her way up the narrow inlets, the captain navigating by compass, experience–always experience–and the echoes of her whistle from the surrounding mountains. Memories of huge waves rolling in from the endless Pacific toward the unforgiving coast of Vancouver Island where, from the steamer's deck, above the howling wind, you could hear the waves breaking at night. Or of the warmth of the cabins as winter-chilled rains lashed the coast from Jordan River to Cape Scott for seemingly endless days without interruption. And perhaps, and ironically, if you were Nuu-Chah-Nulth, of sitting in second class or on the freight deck on the way to a cannery to process the salmon that once and for thousands of years had been yours alone. For the Nuu-Chah-Nulth, other First Nations, Chinese and Japanese passengers, travel on the *Princesses* and other coastal liners improved over the years but was underlain by an apparently unwritten, but nonetheless real, racial or socio-economic separation. Most went second-class or stayed on the freight deck. In later years the social barriers were less evident and First Peoples felt somewhat more at ease travelling in the main lounges or in taking a stateroom on the coastal vessels.

Chief Earl Maquinna George remembers the Princess Maquinna...
"The passenger and freight steamer *Princess Maquinna* plowed the waters all the way from Vancouver to come across to Victoria, picking up passengers. In the summer months tourists came from all over the world, lots from overseas, Europe and England. It was a CPR-run ferry boat doing business with rich people to come see what the West Coast was like.

"There was first class, second class and third class. In second class you could be in the smoking room section which was the stern end; kind of a large sitting room called a smoking room. The first class was down below. They had staterooms for first class. They also had a sitting room on the upper deck for the first class so there was a place for the rich people, for the middle class and a place also for the poorer people like the Indians and the Chinese. They were placed down with chickens, the pigs, the cows, and all the animals... even the rabbits and the goats. There's these shipments that were coming up from places around the coast for people who wanted to raise these types of animals for use on farms. They stopped every place on the coast: Victoria, Port Alberni, Nitinat, Ohiat, Kildonan, Port Alberni, Ucluelet, Tofino, Kakawis, Ahousaht, Hesquiat, Nootka, fish canneries at Ceepeecee, fish canneries up Nootka Inlet, Zeballos, on to Kyuquot, being the last stop on the coastline in later years. It packed passengers and freight, all kinds of freight.

"There was Capt. Gillam and other well known mariners. That freight boat, the CPR boat, ran the coastline right up until after the war years. It was useful because there were no roads; there were no roads from Port Alberni to Tofino. There were roads from Nanaimo to Port Alberni but the rest of the coastline was quite isolated. The boat was the only way you found out about the outside world; they sold newspapers on it: the *Vancouver Sun, Province*, the *Post-Intelligencer*, comics and magazines."

–CHIEF EARL MAQUINNA GEORGE, HEREDITARY CHIEF OF AHOUSAHT, SPEAKING WITH NANCY TURNER, MAY 1996.

The Not-so-Tranquil West Coast

"Ceepeecee, I will never forget that, because, by the time we got there, they had the dog [chum] salmon packed, cases and cases of it, and so for the first time that year, the *Maquinna* had to open up the midship hold. The deck machine for that hold was right over our stateroom. And it would shake the fillings out of our teeth when they would run that winch! We got to Ceepeecee in the morning, early, because that's what woke me, it was the sound of that winch; it must have been about six o'clock. We stayed there 'til three in the afternoon, and still hadn't gotten all the stuff yet. Captain Carthew said, 'Well, we've got to go on, now, but we will stop here on the way back and load the rest of it.' So, with that they buttoned down the hatch and away we went to the other calls. We went into Kyuquot Sound and made calls there, and finally we got up to Chamiss Bay. [Service north of Chamiss Bay was discontinued in October 1946.] We got back eventually to Ceepeecee and they worked all day, loading that salmon.

"The crew was very happy that the damn ship was full to the gunwales, with that dog salmon in cases, so she was good and heavy. The ship really didn't roll too badly, but she'd go up those tremendous swells and then down. Standing on the boat deck, first you could see clear to Japan, and the next minute, all you could see beside you was a wall of water! And, talk about a ship that could give her own version! She squeaked and groaned in every joint.

"The First Mate came down, when I was at the Purser's office, and he said, 'The Captain says, if you'd like to come up to the wheelhouse, this is a good time to come.' I'm never one to turn down an invitation for that. We got up on that deck, and I thought I was going to be blown overboard; they had no inside passage to the wheelhouse. Off in the distance we could see the Estevan Point light, but we never seemed to get any nearer to it. As we moved along, the light seemed to be going along too! They had throttled the ship down–she wasn't making her full 10 knots or whatever she could do–so at midnight, it came time to change the watch. By this time it was blowing so hard that the Captain didn't want to risk sending the men up to relieve the watch. He told them they weren't going to change the watch until it calmed or we got inside [the sound]. Finally, the light began to look like it actually was coming closer. Then it looked like it was going to be abeam, and it seemed to be abeam for ages. We knew once we got beyond the light we could make a turn to port, and get inside, and so before the ship made its turn, somehow Captain Carthew got up to the wheelhouse, even though he wouldn't let any of the other crew come up.

"When he made the turn and started in to Clayoquot Sound, I thought I would die. I looked out the front of the wheelhouse and there were great big rocks, all around, with the sea breaking over them. And the wind began to slack, immediately that we made the turn, but of course the sea was running and breaking over those big rocks, and I thought 'how in the hell are we going to get in through one of those narrow passages with those big rocks?'

"Capt. Carthew was saying... 'Port five... Hold her right steady there... ease her off a little bit there to your right.' Just as calm as he could be. We went through a place that looked to me like it was far too narrow, between two of the biggest, ugliest rocks I have ever seen in my life! Of course the minute we were inside, why the ship calmed down, and we went on about our business."

–Commodore Lester G. Arellanes, recalling his travels on the Maquinna shortly before her retirement.

The cannery and reduction plant at Ceepeecee were in the sheltered "inside" waters of Esperanza Inlet. –B.C. Government photo, Ken Gibson collection

Roaring Twenties, New Night Boats and the Depression

AS THE 1920S DREW TO A CLOSE pressure for improving automobile service to Vancouver Island continued to grow and the aging *Princess Victoria* underwent a major rebuilding, extending her life and giving her a new role on the Coast. The *Vic* was still in good condition and Troup and CPR management saw several possibilities for her: as an automobile ferry and night boat between Victoria and Seattle as well as a relief for the *Princess Elaine*.[38] What prompted the reconstruction, however, which had been rejected just a few years before, was competition in the form of an old vessel named the *City of Victoria,* an 1893 veteran tracing her ancestry to the Old Bay Line on Chesapeake Bay, which was placed in service between Edmonds, Washington, and Victoria in 1929 by the Edmonds-Victoria Ferry Company. After lengthy consideration, the CPR decided to rebuild the *Vic* over the winter of 1929-30 widening her and renovating her entire passenger accommodations. A large automobile deck was created, giving space for about 50-60 cars, the dining room enlarged to seat 80 people, was relocated as were some of the staterooms, and a verandah cafe and smoking room was built at the after end of the promenade deck. The reconstruction increased her beam from 40 feet, 6 inches (12.4 m) to 57 feet, 6 inches (17.5 m) and the cost was approximately $250,000.

The next summer the *Vic* and the *City of Victoria* were in direct competition for the automobile trade between the Seattle area and Victoria and, of course, the *Marguerite* and *Kathleen* were in summer service on the Triangle Route, also carrying automobiles. Lloyd Stadum served on the *City of Victoria* as fourth cook and recalled the rivalry between the two steamers. Both were scheduled to arrive in Victoria at 10:00 p.m. and each evening, the *Vic* eased past the *City of Victoria* between Foulweather Bluff and Marrowstone Point as the two steamers headed north. "This added insult to injury as the resulting swells from her wake made our top-heavy craft roll unmercifully. In the galley, we had to keep a good watch on our pots and pans to keep them in place. The waiters would have accidents in the dining room, and some passengers would complain about being shaken up a bit."[39]

At the end of the 1930 season, the *City of Victoria* was ready to challenge her rival. As the *Vic* slowly closed on the *City of Victoria*, the Edmonds ferry put on all possible speed and slowly pulled ahead. No one knows how seriously the captain of the *Vic* took this challenge, but the *City of Victoria* kept her lead across Juan de Fuca Strait and passed Brotchie Ledge ahead of the CPR steamer. But the triumph was short-lived because the next day, when the *City of Victoria* was leaving Victoria, the stress on the machinery became all too clear: the old steamer broke down twice on her return to Edmonds, being passed by the

Aging competitors: the *City of Victoria*, above, and the *Princess Victoria*, at right. The *Princess Vic* was about to be rebuilt as an automobile ferry. –VICTOR LOMAS, RBCM; JAMES TURNER PHOTO, CLINTON BETZ COLLECTION

The Princess Victoria after 20 years...
"The C.P.R. British Columbia Coast Service S.S. *Princess Victoria* completed 20 years of service in Pacific coast waters recently. During that time, she travelled over 1,500,000 miles [2,410,000 km] and made 5,197 trips between Vancouver, Victoria and Seattle."
     –*Canadian Railway & Marine World*, FEBRUARY 1923.

Modernizing the Princess Victoria, 1929...
"There will be hot and cold running water throughout the ship [which had not previously been provided], and she will be generally stiffer; by that I mean with less vibration. The dance floor will be inside aft, above the dining room. Note the extensive promenade in the alley-ways abaft the observation room, and the spacious dining-room the full width of the ship. The accommodation for large cars is about 56. ...it is proposed to overhaul the entire stateroom accommodation to remove squeaks, and rattles."
     –CAPT. NEROUTSOS TO N. R. DESBRISAY, GENERAL PASSENGER AGENT, VANCOUVER, JUNE 5, 1929.

afternoon *Princess* at high speed. This effectively brought an end to the *City of Victoria's* service. Perhaps the most beneficial aspect of the service was that it prompted the reconstruction of the *Princess Victoria* and, as a result, prolonged her life. As events were to unfold, the *Vic* would prove a very valuable member of the fleet, particularly in the busy wartime years of the 1940s.

The succession of new steamers delivered to the B.C. Coast Steamship Service seemed endless during the prosperous 1920s and as the *Princess Norah* was taking form at the Fairfield yards, two large passenger steamers designed specially for the Victoria–Vancouver night boat service were under development by the CPR. These were the last Coast Service vessels to have Capt. Troup's distinctive input in their design but he retired before they entered service, his position being taken over by Capt. Cyril Neroutsos who had served for many years as Assistant Manager under Troup and had long experience on the Pacific Coast.

These two steamers, each of 5,251 tons and 366 feet (112 m) in length by 52 feet (15.8 m) in breadth, were fitted with 185 staterooms providing a total of 341 berths each. Their day certificates were for 1,100 passengers. Dining room capacity was 66 and coffee shop seating was 34. Two large quadruple-expansion engines, driving twin screws, produced efficient, vibration-free operation but speed was limited to 16.5 knots (19 miles or 30.5 km an hour). They could carry about 50 automobiles as well as large volumes of freight loaded onto

The *Princess Victoria* after her extensive reconstruction retained many of her signature features including her pilot house and three funnels but the sponsoning of her hull gave her a much wider hull and left her looking more functional than elegant when viewed from the bow. —CYRIL LITTLEBURY, AT LEFT, AND ALBERT H. PAULL, ABOVE, AUTHOR'S COLLECTION

The new dining room on the *Princess Victoria* was spacious and reflected the simplified decor popular in the late 1920s. —CANADIAN PACIFIC

The Princess Joan and Princess Elizabeth, Trials completed...
"Just returned from the trial trip of the *Joan*, 16.9 knots [19.4 miles or 31.3 km an hour], running like a charm, no smoke, full power about 3900 [horsepower]. Oil temp 105°, pressure 108 lbs, no vibration anywhere. That's that."

—CAPT. CYRIL NEROUTSOS TO SUPERINTENDENT ENGINEER
    J. H. ALEXANDER, APRIL 5, 1930.

The new night boats, the *Princess Joan* and *Princess Elizabeth* (often called the "Lizzie") introduced in 1930, were stately and relatively slow but they became favourites of many travellers between Vancouver, Victoria and Seattle over careers that lasted nearly 30 years. —MAURICE CHANDLER

pallets on the main deck. Various builders in Great Britain submitted quotations but the reliable Fairfield yards won the contract late in 1928 with a total price of £420,100 for the steamers, which were named the *Princess Joan* and the *Princess Elizabeth*.

The stock market collapse on Wall Street in 1929 was already having its impact on the world economy and the CPR was lucky that it had begun work on these vessels because they were to be exceptionally economical and useful vessels over a career that lasted nearly 30 years. They were the last major additions to the fleet until after the Second World War. "These ships thanks to the assistance that I have had from yourself and others on this side are without a doubt the most completely satisfactory of the whole fleet," wrote Capt. Neroutsos on April 5, 1930. "Our men cannot cease commenting on them, and we have also a very economical job, the lack of water disturbance at full speed is beyond your conception, in fact at 16.5 knots they are like the *Adelaide* at 13 knots [15 miles or 24 km an hour]."[40] Their large passenger capacity and economy of operation prompted their use on the daylight services of the Triangle Route even though they were designed primarily for the night runs. Moreover, from the beginning of their service they were also used on the Vancouver to-Nanaimo service with either of the night boats often making one daylight return sailing a day. They proved popular vessels with the public and were an enduring feature of the Seattle, Victoria, Vancouver and Nanaimo waterfronts for decades.

Inaugural Luncheon

COMMEMORATING THE INITIAL SAILING
OF THE TWIN-SCREW
PASSENGER STEAMER

S.S. Princess Joan

OPERATING BETWEEN
NANAIMO *and* VANCOUVER
DAILY

NANAIMO · 27TH JUNE, 1930

HORS D'OEUVRES

—

CRABMEAT COCKTAIL

—

CONSOMME ROYAL

—

GRILLED CHICKEN WATERCRESS
FRESH MUSHROOMS
GREEN PEAS
O'BRIEN POTATOES
ICED ASPARAGUS

—

PRINCESS ICES

—

COFFEE

Luncheon Menu. –AUTHOR'S COLLECTION

The stately *Princess Elizabeth* captured by master photographer Joe D. Williamson off Seattle in 1959. At right, the *Elizabeth* at dock side and an onboard view of one of the sisterships passing under the Lions Gate Bridge. –JOE D. WILLIAMSON, LORNE CAMPBELL COLLECTION; DR. W. B. CHUNG COLLECTION; AND ALBERT H. PAULL, AUTHOR'S COLLECTION

The Night Boats, fondly recalled...

"They rocked a bit on windy nights; but what matter when we had an implicit faith (seldom shaken) that by 7:00 a.m.—come hell or high water—we would be tied up safe in port. They travelled by the deep sea channels, along the International Boundary, so there was no problem negotiating Active Pass on murky nights.

"When there is a particularly heavy gale blowing, my wife and I say to each other, 'This would be a good night to be catching the night boat.'"

–TOM GOODLAKE, PURSER.

Those Midnight Boats...

When we got on the boat for our Honeymoon, to come over to Vancouver, we went out on deck to wave to all the people who [came to see us off and] were down below on the dock. The first guy who came along and met us was Don's boss, which is not what you want on your Honeymoon. But he was very tactful. He just said congratulations and a few words and departed."

–PHYLLIS HORNE.

"He was a real gentleman."

–DON HORNE.

But not an Inside Stateroom...

"Those boats were lovely unless you got an inside stateroom. One time we were going over with Donna when she was very small. Not having much money, we paid for one of the cheapest staterooms which didn't have a window. It just opened to the inside. It was the biggest mistake of our lives! We put her in the bottom bunk, because she wasn't old enough to go up the top. We were up the top. It was so hot it was unbelievable! We didn't stay in it. We sat up all night and kept going outside to get a breath of air. No air conditioning, no window and a little tiny room about the size of a small bathroom."

–PHYLLIS HORNE.

The *Elizabeth*, the "midnight boat," ready to sail from Victoria. –EARL J. MARSH COLLECTION

The Depression of the 1930s idled many vessels and reduced services on some routes but only the oldest vessels in the CPR fleet, due for retirement after the arrival of newer *Princesses*, were sold. The imminent retirement and scrapping of the older vessels caused some problems in reorganizing the fleet. The *Princess Mary*, used primarily on the North Coast route, was the only vessel suitable for taking over from the *Royal* which was temporarily on the Powell River, Gulf Islands routes. This left a void and the *Adelaide*, idle much of the time since the arrival of the *Joan* and *Elizabeth*, was the only vessel available. However, the *Adelaide* was larger, more expensive to operate and was not designed to carry significant quantities of cargo. Moreover, her accommodations were intended for short overnight trips, not voyages of several days or a week in duration and the staterooms were small and without wardrobes. After considerable deliberation, the CPR decided to spend $30,000 to modify the *Adelaide* for this service and she was to operate up the Coast for almost two more decades. The alterations included the removal of the lunch counter and, most importantly, an expansion of cargo capacity and a rearrangement of crew's quarters and of the second class passenger accommodations.[41]

In 1932, with the economy at an unprecedented low, several fine steamers spent more time out of service than in operation. For example, the *Louise*, just a decade old, was only in commission 123 days, the *Alice* was running just 161 days and the *Charlotte* was laid up for nearly five months. But the *Joan* and *Elizabeth*, economical to operate and surprisingly versatile were out of service just seven and eight days respectively; just long enough for maintenance. Other stalwarts, including the *Mary, Maquinna, Adelaide, Norah* and *Elaine* ran regularly throughout the year. The *Marguerite* and *Kathleen*, because of their high operating costs, slept out the winter months of low traffic at the Victoria docks. Older vessels including the *Vic*, the *Royal* in its very last year of operation and the *Pat* spent most of their days out of service finding useful work only in the summer months or as relief vessels.[42]

The *Royal* was sold for scrap in 1933 and the *Patricia* followed in 1937. The old *Beatrice*, never modernized to burn oil like all the other passenger-carrying *Princesses*, had already been sold in the late 1920s. An insight into the *Royal's* long and successful career comes from her final accounting. She cost the company $280,270 in 1907. The net revenues from her operations over the next 26 years were $863,737.87, yielding a return to the company of $679,866.65 which reflected a modest return on investment averaging just under 12 percent a year. Moreover, there were additional revenues received from traffic, made possible by her services, that was carried on the railway to and from Vancouver or on the *Empress* liners in trans-Pacific service.[43]

Newcastle Island

STEAMSHIP EXCURSIONS WERE POPULAR FOR PEOPLE all along the Pacific Coast but by the 1920s, the CPR found itself at a disadvantage in attracting this valuable traffic. The Union Steamship Company, based in Vancouver, provided stiff competition with its very popular excursions to its popular resort on Bowen Island and other destinations. As a response in 1930, the CPR purchased 754-acre (305-ha) Newcastle Island just off Nanaimo from the Western Fuel Company and developed extensive picnic grounds with dance pavilion, restaurant, playing field and other facilities for an initial investment of about $80,000.[44] The CPR hoped that the facilities would attract additional passengers on its regular sailings during the summer months, as well as encourage group charters and special trips. These were particularly valuable to the company, which used the *Princess Patricia*, no longer needed on the Vancouver–Nanaimo service, for excursions, and it was also possible to use other steamers, such as the night boats, to good advantage between their regular runs. Newcastle Island, as a CPR facility, was opened on June 20, 1931 when the *Princess Victoria* brought a large group from Vancouver.

During the Depression years of the 1930s the *Charmer* and *Princess Victoria*, both out of service, were moored at Newcastle Island and people were able to rent staterooms on board for vacations. Cooking facilities were provided and they were a pleasant, unusual and inexpensive option for family holidays. The *Charmer* was scrapped after her Newcastle days but the *Vic* returned to service as economic conditions improved. In 1941, with the increasing pressures of the war, the CPR ended service to Newcastle Island but briefly reopened the facilities in 1950. Later the property was sold to the city of Nanaimo which in 1960 transferred it to the Provincial Government as a park.

Newcastle Excursions returned after the War...
"We would take from Vancouver, perhaps the employees of Woodward's Department store. Then we would dock at Newcastle Island, which was a stone's throw from downtown Nanaimo and deposit the people. After a trip or two back to Vancouver, we would pick them up again and take them home to Vancouver."

–J. GARY RICHARDSON, STEWARD, RECALLING THE POST-WAR YEARS OF THE BCCSS.

Choice of
White or Brown Bread Toast
Devilled Egg or Salmon Sandwich
Toasted Buns or Muffins
Madeira or Princess Fruit Cake
Strawberry Jam   Canadian Honey
Tea, Hot or Iced
Ice Cream may be substituted for Tea

AT ONE OF NEWCASTLE ISLAND'S BEACHES

–DR. W. B. CHUNG COLLECTION

Newcastle Island remained popular despite the Depression and the *Princess Victoria* and *Charmer* were both used as accommodations for vacationers. However, for the antiquated and frail old *Charmer* there would be no lasting reprieve. She was sold and scrapped in Victoria in 1935. The scene above shows the two steamers at the long Newcastle Island wharf. –ALBERT H. PAULL AUTHOR'S COLLECTION

"New Vacation Thrill..."

"This is a vacation that will live in your memory at a price everyone can afford to pay. You may have a two-berth upper deck room, fully furnished for as low as $5.00 per week, including towels, and running water. Meals can be secured at the Pavilion Verandah Restaurant at moderate rates, or the facilities of the ship's gallery are at the disposal of those who wish to prepare their own meals. Provisions may be brought with you or purchased at the Pavilion.

"The appointments of the *Princess Victoria* are complete in every detail. You have your own bathing house on board ship, and for those who wish to dance, the ship's ballroom is always available.

"A stewardess will be in charge of the *Princess Victoria* and she will be glad to assist in any way possible."

–NEWCASTLE ISLAND BROCHURE, CA. 1935, EARL J. MARSH COLLECTION

The *Princess Victoria* returned to service after her stint as an accommodation ship at Newcastle Island. She continued to bring thousands of people to the resort for picnics and excursions and was kept busy on the Triangle Route and other inter-city services during the Second World War. –CLINTON BETZ

Of Dreams and Letters Home

Postcard of the *Princess Victoria* to Maude, Portage la Prairie, Manitoba....
March 1906
This is my yacht on which I tour the world in my Dreams.
H.E.B.

❧ ❧ ❧

Postcard to Miss Weiss, Westmoreland, Pennsylvania...
On board the Princess Victoria
Aug. 8, 1907
Dear Pat—
This is the steamer I'm on—and we are nearing Vancouver. It is fine! How I wish you were on to enjoy it. Water nice... R.

❧ ❧ ❧

Postcard to Ada, South Oxford, Nova Scotia...
November 25, 1908
Dear Ada....
This [the Princess Victoria] *is the steamer on which Art was on board. It is very elegant!.... Love Jim.*

❧ ❧ ❧

Postcard of a new *Princess Charlotte* to Master H. H. Miller, New Westminster....
March 25, 1908 or 1909
This is the boat I and Ana came down on, it is lovely. She is in the dry dock now getting ready for the summer. Hope you are a good boy. Kiss from your loving Mother.

❧ ❧ ❧

Postcard from Alert Bay....
S/S Princess Alice
July 12, 1912
Have had a dandy trip so far.
The scenery is great. Very nice crowd aboard.
Stew.

Young Earl writes home...
Vancouver
March 30, 1914
Dear Dad,
Arrived here O.K. Everybody on the boat was sea sick but me and I was D–Sick. Do you gather me. D–sick, sick, sick. Earl.

Card to Laura, Cape May, New Jersey...
Juneau, Alaska
July 13, 1928
This is the steamer [the Princess Alice] we are going to Alaska on. We left Vancouver Wed. 9 p.m. and now will shortly be at Ketchikan. Wonderful trip—all well. Beautiful scenery. We arrive back in Victoria next Wed.   J.M.

Postcard to Victoria from Vancouver...
August 10, 1933
Dear Isabella,
We had a nice trip on the boat [Princess Marguerite or Kathleen]. We have been to Stanley Park and we are going to see a movie tonight.   Audrey.

An Unsigned postcard of the *Princess Kathleen*, about 1935, from a young writer...
Dear Rick,
This is the passenger liner I rode on to Victoria and Vancouver, Canada. On the boat I met Spencer Tracy on his vacation. He is a nervous guy and did not want to be seen but I saw him plenty of times. I went in the Empress Hotel in Victoria. It is the biggest hotel in the Northwest.

Postcard of Ocean Falls...
Mrs. J. M. O., Kansas City
August 17, 1938
This will be our first stop. Will report later if it really looks this way. Grand cool weather. Just coming out of a heavy mist. Clouds down below Mt. peaks making scenery very lovely. We all have to report for Emergency Drill in a few minutes. Put on life belt and all. Then on to "Horse races" Grand crowd. Nice boat.   Emily.

Postcard to West Marpawell, Maine...
Victoria, July 29, 1941
This afternoon the car was put on this boat [Princess Victoria] and we had a 2 1/2 hr. trip to Nanaimo (Na-ní-mo) then drive 78 miles to Victoria. Beautiful sail and drive. Tomorrow afternoon we take another boat to Anacortes, Wash. U.S.A.! N.D.P.

Postcard of the *Princess Kathleen*, ca. 1935...
The boat we were on for the day on Puget Sound—a beautiful trip. The water so smooth. The boat so comfortable and our stay in Victoria (B.C.) and the hour ride around this city (on an island) was lovely. We stayed at Vancouver (B.C.) and took the night train for the Canadian Rockies & Lake Louise & Banff.

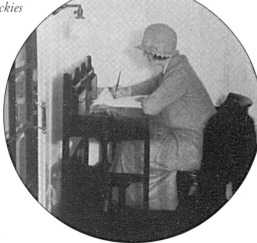

Fortunately conditions along the coast improved as the 1930s drew to a close. The BCCSS was operating a still-modern fleet of steamers on the following routes, as shown in the summer schedule for 1938:

-Vancouver-Victoria-Seattle, Triangle Route, double daily service by the *Princess Kathleen* and *Princess Marguerite*. There was additional daily midnight boat service from Victoria and Vancouver by the *Princess Joan* and *Princess Elizabeth* and a second Victoria-to-Seattle return trip by either the *Princess Joan* or *Princess Elizabeth*.

-Vancouver-Nanaimo, three sailings a day, with four on Saturdays and Sundays, using primarily the *Princess Elaine* and *Princess Victoria* but with additional trips by the *Princess Joan* or *Princess Elizabeth*. One sailing a day from Vancouver also stopped at the CPR's Newcastle Island picnic facilities just off Nanaimo; two trips were made there on Sundays.

-West Coast of Vancouver Island, from Victoria to Port Alice, with as many as 18 stops along the way, on a weekly service with the *Princess Norah*. In addition, the *Princess Maquinna* ran weekly trips, on a complementary schedule, from Victoria to Zeballos, with as many as 27 ports of call or boat landings.

-Alaska Service, from Vancouver with stops at Alert Bay, Ketchikan, Wrangell, Taku Glacier, Juneau and Skagway, sailings about once a week, and more frequently in July and August, alternating between the *Princess Louise*, *Princess Alice* and *Princess Charlotte*.

-Vancouver to Ocean Falls and Prince Rupert, with 10 stops, on a weekly schedule provided by the *Princess Adelaide*.

-Vancouver to Powell River and Comox, with stops at Comox, Union Bay and Hornby, Denman and Texada islands, three times a week by the *Princess Mary*.

-Gulf Islands Service, with one trip from Vancouver through to Victoria and return over two days; one return trip Vancouver to Ganges and way ports by the *Princess Mary*. In addition the *Motor Princess* made one trip from Sidney via Port Washington, Ganges, Mayne Island and Galiano to Vancouver.

-Steveston-Sidney, direct service for automobiles, two return trips Monday through Saturday; one trip Sundays, with the *Motor Princess*.

Passenger volumes, freight and automobile traffic recovered and showed growth. In 1938 the service handled 63,531 automobiles, up substantially from the 40,440 carried in 1929 and the low of 27,886 carried in 1932. Year-end returns for 1938 showed that 878,000 passengers and 146,000 tons of freight had been carried. Moreover, the tug and transfer barge service between Vancouver and the Esquimalt & Nanaimo Railway on Vancouver Island carried 256,696 railway cars.

Reflecting the changing nature of travel on the Coast, the Puget Sound Navigation Company's *Iroquois*, rebuilt as a car ferry, contrasts with the *Marguerite* at Victoria in 1935. The Coast Service's tug and railcar barge fleet was an important but little noticed part of its operations. The main railcar transfer slips were located at Vancouver, just west of the passenger steamer piers, and at Ladysmith and Nanoose Bay on Vancouver Island. This photo from May 29, 1929, shows the charter tug *Point Ellice* and the CPR's *Qualicum*, *Nanoose* and *Dola* at Vancouver. –NORMAN GIDNEY; ALBERT H. PAULL, AUTHOR'S COLLECTION

Capt. Cyril Demetrius Neroutsos and later Managers...

Capt. Neroutsos became manager of the BCCSS on September 1, 1928, following the retirement of Capt. Troup. Neroutsos, who had worked with Troup since 1901, was very familiar with the operations and requirements of the service. He had been appointed assistant manager in June 1925. Born on March 18, 1868 in Bowdon, Cheshire, England, to a Greek father and an English mother, Neroutsos started at sea on sailing vessels in August 1882 at little more than 14 years of age. He joined the Canadian Pacific Navigation Company at the time of the CPR takeover of the coastal steamship operation and served on many vessels, rising from first mate to master. In 1911 he became marine superintendent.

Neroutsos' tenure as manager was brief and he retired in 1934. Remembered as a capable administrator, like Troup, he spent his entire working life dealing with ships and shipping concerns. In the 1920s, he travelled to Scotland on several occasions to oversee the details of construction for new *Princesses*. Earl Marsh remembered the Captain coming through into the office and shouting for people. "He could be the personification of Capt. Bligh," recalled Earl with a laugh, remembering his days as a young accountant in the Victoria headquarters, "but he was kindhearted." His Greek surname notwithstanding, he was, as Martin Lynch recalled, very British in his demeanor, and "tough and leathery."

Capt. Neroutsos lived in retirement in Victoria, firing a small canon each noon in his garden, and was frequently called "the Skipper." He died in December 1954 at age 86. Like James Troup, ships and the sea had been his whole life. He was survived by his son, Cyril H. Neroutsos and daughter Mrs. H. W. Blenkinsop.

Neroutsos' successor was Capt. R. W. McMurray who served as manager from 1934 until 1945 when he was promoted to managing director of Canadian Pacific Steamships and moved to Montreal. Capt. Oliver J. Williams, who was marine superintendent in Vancouver between 1940 and 1945, became manager in July 1945 and he remained in charge of the fleet through the troubled postwar years until he retired in 1962. Harry Tyson took over and managed the fleet until 1973. His successors with Canadian Pacific included H. L. Thompson, Barry Margetts, James Yates, Mike Holland, Victor Jones, Ray Purdy, Al Cairns and finally Alec MacPherson.

B.C. Coast Service People....

Chief Engineer John A. Heritage

Capt. Claude Clifford Sainty

Chief Cook Wong Gin Wo

Capt. Oliver J. Williams, Manager

H. W. Marshall, Vancouver Shops, and Supt. Engineer Hugh Tumilty

Capt. L. C. Barry, O.B.E.

Sixth Engineer William B. Harris, M.B.E., *Princess Marguerite*

Freight Clerk Jack Lenfesty, in 1946, later Assistant Purser

Hostess Gladys Sherman

The Inside Passage...

"Along nearly 1,000 miles [1600 km] of the most picturesque coastline in the world lies the scenic 'Inside Passage' to Skagway. Past deep fjords where the mountains rise straight from the sea, by beautiful inlets carpeted with heavy timber, your Princess steamer sails serenely towards the land of the Midnight Sun."

–Canadian Pacific B.C. Coast Steamships, Alaska and the Yukon, 1941.

Stewards on the *Princess Alice* in the Lynn Canal during an Alaska cruise in the 1920s: W. A. Williams, Harry Cooper, Pat Playne, two unidentified stewards, Charles Edwards and Bill Noakes. –Earl Marsh collection

The sale of First Nations' and Native American basketry and carvings was an important attraction on the Alaska and Vancouver Island services. Insightful travellers appreciated the artistry and quality of the work. Many pieces sold on the docks are now highly prized and in world-renowned collections. The artists often dressed to appeal to the tourists. –CPR brochure, 1931

At left, the *Princess Charlotte*, the Pacific Coast Steamship Company's *Alameda* and the Canadian National's *Prince Robert* are at the Skagway wharf on a beautiful clear summer day in the 1930s. –Dedman's Photo Shop

Alaska Service

THE ALASKA SERVICE WAS ONE OF THE PREMIER CPR ROUTES. However, traffic varied greatly with the seasons and normally large vessels could not pay their way in the stormy winter months when there was little passenger traffic. By the 1930s and through the 1940s, the B.C. Coast Steamship Service normally operated the *Princess Alice*, *Princess Charlotte* and *Princess Louise* on the route with the *Princess Norah* being the primary vessel during the winter. The *Alice* and the *Charlotte* usually returned to Triangle Route duties during the winter when the larger and more expensive-to-operate *Princess Kathleen* and *Princess Marguerite* were laid up.

The Alaska run, highlighted by beautiful scenery and the romance of the Klondike Gold Rush, was perennially popular and a growing destination for travellers. Several other shipping lines were active in the trade including the Alaska Steamship Company, the Pacific Coast Steamship Company and Canadian National Railways. A gentleman's agreement prevailed between the shipping lines with an understanding that no one would try to monopolize the route or get into unprofitable cost-cutting competition and that fares would be kept within a mutually-acceptable range.

In the early days of the Coast Service, business to Skagway was brisk in the aftermath of the Klondike Gold Rush. By the 1920s, however, tourists travelling on the Alaska route had become a very important source of revenue not only to the Coast Steamship Service but also for the railway and, because they often travelled by CPR trains and stopped along the way at Banff and Lake Louise, to the CPR Hotels in the Rocky Mountains.

Skagway was the northern terminus of the CPR's Alaska service and a highlight of the summer cruises. Passengers could transfer to the White Pass & Yukon's narrow gauge railway for the journey to Whitehorse. From there they could travel by sternwheeler down the Yukon River to Dawson, the centre of the Klondike mining region. Alternately, from Carcross on the White Pass & Yukon, tourists could take the sternwheeler *Tutshi* for a cruise on Tagish Lake or perhaps visit Atlin. Business to and from the Yukon remained important to the financial success of the Alaska service but the passenger traffic of the summer months provided critical revenue. The scheduled stops were at Alert Bay, Prince Rupert, Ketchikan, Wrangell, Juneau and Skagway. A nine-day "Princess Cruise" was priced as low as $105 in the early 1940s. An extended 11-day cruise on the *Princess Charlotte*, which included a stop Sitka, cost from $125.00 for a berth in a shared stateroom. More spacious accommodations cost as much as $420 for two people in the ship's largest stateroom, which provided two single berths, a sofa berth, shower and private toilet.

A Quartet to Alaska and a String Trio on the Triangle Route...

"We only did two dance sessions on each trip to Alaska. We played about five luncheons and about two dinners. I was playing cello. We had a violin, cello and piano and a clarinet or sax. On the Triangle run, on the *Kathleen*, we just had three; we had a string trio, a violin, cello and piano. We would have a steady routine. We'd leave Seattle at 9:00 o'clock and we'd play in the morning to Victoria. And then about the same thing in the afternoon. We'd leave Victoria and we'd play for an hour, an hour and a half, before we'd be in Vancouver. Then we had the evening in Vancouver and got on the ship before 11:00 and be overnight to Seattle. With the *Marguerite*, their routine was exactly the opposite. They'd have their evenings in Seattle and then overnight to Vancouver and then play Vancouver to Victoria and Victoria to Seattle. I was on the boats between 1934 and '37."

—Glen Stewart Morley, musician, BCCSS.

Scenes from the Alaska service: The *Princess Alice* at Skagway; the *Louise* at Taku Glacier and the *Charlotte* at Alert Bay. At right, the *Adelaide* steams by through the sheltered Inside Passage on her North Coast service in the 1930s.
–F. L. Pedersen photo, Yukon Archives 3165; Ordway photo, Author's collection; and Fred Wanstall photos

Coastal Navigation and Foggy Foggy Nights...

"I have been on the night boat leaving Victoria when the fog was so dense you could hardly see 20 feet [5 or 6 m], but with considerable blowing of the whistle, listening for the echo and for the fog horns, we slowly made our way out into the Gulf...

"I recall many years ago during a period of dense fog which lasted for eight or 10 days when the ships operated on the Triangle and between Vancouver and Victoria, navigated for at least a week without having been able to see more than a few feet ahead at any time. The strain ultimately became so great on these men that Capt. Troup... cancelled the service until the fog lifted.

"During foggy weather, the whistle, where an echo can be obtained, is used very extensively. A ship, for instance, going from Vancouver to Victoria on a foggy night, when she gets into the Gulf of Georgia knows that a certain time ordinarily will elapse before contact is made with the islands off Vancouver Island [the Gulf Islands]. The whistle, therefore, is sounded and as they are familiar with the topography of the land en route, they are able to estimate from the echo, based on the speed which sounds make, how close they are to shore and a particular shore which, of course, is important. This echo, when the topography of the land is suitable, not only enables them to tell whether land is ahead, but how close on either side the shore may be. The whistle, with its resulting echo, is a great aid to navigators during foggy or thick weather."

–C. E. STOCKDILL, ASSISTANT TO VICE-PRESIDENT, CPR, FEBRUARY 20, 1940.[45]

One day early in 1943, the *Princess Norah* steamed out of the fog that hung over the Lynn Canal and arrived at Skagway like a ghostly apparition, shrouded in ice. For the crew there was little alternative but to begin chipping it off. But the deck cargo could not be unloaded and had to be returned to Vancouver. Steamers and their crews also had to battle winter storms and each winter, even in the sheltered waters of the Gulf of Georgia and Puget Sound, gales could blow up with heavy seas that would prompt all but the best seafaring passengers to shun the dining rooms of the *Princesses*. At right, the *Kathleen* or *Marguerite* takes seas right over her pilot house. At other times fog could blanket the coast for days at a time. –LORNE CAMPBELL COLLECTION; MILTON BRALEY COLLECTION

The *Princess Adelaide*, in a beautiful portrait at Prince Rupert, spent her last decades on the North Coast route calling at Campbell River, Englewood, Alert Bay, Port Hardy, Namu, Ocean Falls, Butedale and Prince Rupert. Other ports included canneries and logging camps. The *Adelaide* proved to be one of the most highly utilized vessels in the fleet. –NICHOLAS MORANT, CP ARCHIVES

The *Marguerite,* her Royal Yacht duties completed, and *Kathleen* at Victoria on May 30, 1939, as the King and Queen arrive at the Empress Hotel for the state luncheon. Above left, the King and Queen on the *Marguerite* passing under the Lions Gate Bridge, and at left, Queen Elizabeth on the *Princess Marguerite.* –EARL MARSH COLLECTION

The Royal Visit of 1939

By THE SPRING OF 1939, the world was close to war. In that last spring of peace, King George VI and Queen Elizabeth made the first royal visit to Canada, travelling across the country by special trains in a gala tour that introduced Canadians to their new King following the abdication of Edward VIII and reinforced ties to Britain at a time when support from what was then still called the Empire would be so critical. From Vancouver the Royal party travelled to Victoria on the *Princess Marguerite,* for a brief but well-received visit. With the Royal party aboard, the spotlessly maintained *Marguerite,* under the command of Capt. Clifford Felton, sailed from Pier B-C at 5:00 p.m. on May 29, 1939 and arrived in Victoria, to a 21-gun salute off Ogden Point, four hours later. Arthur Steward was chief steward, Lam Sar Ning and Choy Caow were chief cooks, Alexander Taylor was purser, and Robert Moffat was chief engineer. The *Princess Kathleen* operated on an evening cruise to meet the *Marguerite* in the Gulf Islands and the next day both *Princesses* made special trips from Seattle to Victoria. Schedules were modified to make it easier for people to come to Victoria, the *Alice* made a excursion trip from Vancouver and the *Mary* operated on a special trip from the Gulf Islands on the 30th. On May 30th, a state luncheon was held at the Empress Hotel. The return voyage was on the CNR's *Prince Robert.*

Wartime, Renewal and Change

❧

"*On one trip the boat was full of youngsters, not even 20 years old, who had just joined up. Phyl, Jean and I went over to Vancouver. We were talking to those young guys; they were very excited, having a new adventure. We later found out many of them were on the destroyer* Margaree, *one of them was a neighbour; there were a lot of them who didn't come home. The* Margaree *was sunk.*"

—Isabella Turner.

Secret Memorandum for the Chairman...

"*The following message has been received, through the Naval Service, today:-*

"*Following received from Stuart Begins 543 Admiralty Reports* Princess Marguerite *Sunk all Europeans and Canadians Safe Chinese one dead and five missing.*"

Captain R. A. Leicester, ex our Pacific Steamship Service, was in command of the Princess Marguerite."

—E. Aikman, Assistant to the Chairman, August 25, 1942.

Just over 20 years after the Armistice ending the "War to end all wars," the Second World War began in Europe and Canada once again became committed to years of struggle and hardship. The *Princesses* again carried hundreds of troops and recreated for a younger generation the emotional scenes of departure from Victoria. These young men, probably from Princess Patricia's Canadian Light Infantry, are leaving Victoria aboard the *Princess Elaine*. –Author's collection

CHAPTER 3

The Princesses in Wartime

WHEN WAR BEGAN AGAIN WITH GERMANY in 1939 its impact was soon felt on the Pacific Coast. Young men began showing up in smart new uniforms and the reality of what lay ahead came all too close to home. The shipyards grew very busy, women joined the work force, consumer goods were short in supply, rationing was on the horizon and military training facilities opened in many areas. For the BC Coast Service the greatest impact was in late 1941 when the *Princess Kathleen* and *Princess Marguerite* were requisitioned for service with the British Admiralty in the Mediterranean. The two beautiful *Princesses*, the pride of the Coast Service, left Victoria on November 7, 1941, exactly a month before the Japanese attack on Pearl Harbor.

By the time the two *Princesses* were on their way, 175 of the Coast Service's permanent seagoing staff had joined the armed forces and others had gone to work in local shipyards. Remaining staff were hard pressed to maintain the services let alone provide extra sailings during times of heavy traffic. Nonetheless, in the fall of 1941, there were so many service personnel travelling back and forth between Victoria and Vancouver—often 500 to 600 each weekend—that extra daylight sailings of the night boats had to be operated on the weekends to take care of the servicemen and furlough tickets were stamped "Not good on the midnight boat." Initially, the servicemen, who were not given stateroom tickets on their weekend leave passes, filled every lounge and nook on the midnight boats.

In wartime service the *Princesses* took on an austere coat of grey paint and it changed their appearance from elegant to menacing. Some of them even carried defensive weapons but they were never used except perhaps for practice. The *Princesses* at home remained untouched by the war although on one occasion the *Norah's* sailing to the West Coast of Vancouver Island was delayed when a Japanese submarine shelled the lighthouse at Estevan Point between Ucluelet and Tofino.

The war years took a heavy toll on the aging fleet of *Princesses*. Materials were in short supply as was skilled labour. Through the hectic years of the 1940s, with traffic growing rapidly, the burden of intercity services fell once again on the stalwarts of the fleet: the *Princess Victoria*, *Princess Charlotte*, *Princess Alice* and, in the winter months, the *Princess Louise*. On November 1, 1941 the Vancouver–Seattle night service was suspended. Operated again the next summer, thereafter it was cancelled until summer 1947. Instead, the steamers operated on what was known as the Tri-City service; the vessels stopped at Victoria on all sailings without the direct service between Vancouver and Seattle. The newer *Joan* and *Elizabeth*, intended for night boat services, often ran daylight trips and the *Louise*, intended for the Alaska service, frequently ran on the Triangle Route. The *Joan* and *Elizabeth*, with their large stateroom accommodation, had limited space in their lounges or outside on the decks, so conditions could be crowded during busy daytime runs. The steamers were slow compared with the *Marguerite* and *Kathleen,* and could take five and a half hours on the day run between Victoria and Vancouver, but they were economical to operate.

Sometimes there were so many passengers on the night runs that people were sleeping everywhere, stretched out on the decks, on the floors of the lounges or slumped over in chairs if they were lucky. Suitcases served as seats and parents could spend a long uncomfortable night with small, tired children on their laps for hours. But at the same time most people were uncomplaining, someone would play the piano and there would be impromptu dances and sing-along sessions to pass the time.

The Princess Kathleen & Princess Marguerite at War

THE WORSENING MILITARY SITUATION in Europe and North Africa in 1941 prompted the British Admiralty to requisition the *Princess Kathleen* and *Princess Marguerite*. The charter for each vessel was at a rate of $13,315.53 a month and if lost, the Ministry of National Defense agreed to reimburse the CPR the sum of $1,291,238, payable four-fifths in cash and the balance through the tonnage replacement fund of the Ministry of War Transport. Initially the intention was to convert the ships to fast supply vessels for the Mediterranean and to this end work was carried out on the *Marguerite* at Yarrows in Esquimalt and on the *Kathleen* at the Victoria Machinery Depot. However, they were used primarily as troop ships. They sailed in company from Victoria for Alexandria, Egypt, via the South Pacific. Capt. L.C. Barry was in command of the *Kathleen* and Capt. Richard A. Leicester was master of the *Marguerite*. The two *Princesses* soon ran into heavy weather. The *Kathleen's* voyage report noted "squalls of hurricane force, very high sea and swell, ship pitching and rolling heavily, average speed for the 24 hours being 6 ¼ knots, very little water shipped, but vessel smothered in spray practically all the time." John Whitworth wrote to F. K. Bailey, the superintendent engineer in Victoria, that "We have had heavy seas and howling winds...[and] the ship has done everything but turn over. We had to slow down or we would have been battered all shapes. Down in the engine room everything is running well."

Wartime passages...

"We came over from Victoria and didn't have much money. We weren't going to buy a stateroom; so we sat up all night. It was very entertaining because it was during the war and all the sailors were there. One was playing the piano and everybody was singing. It was a big room with the piano and everybody was loving it. We didn't even feel tired in the morning."

–PHYLLIS HORNE.

Blackout on the Princesses...

"Immediately after Pearl Harbor, the ships had baffles installed at the hatchways to keep light from being visible at night. Smoking on decks was prohibited. There was either a pale blue or red light installed in the baffled area. Blackout curtains were installed on the lounge windows. Piles of life vests were strategically placed along the boat deck. Emergency instructions were posted everywhere."

–KEN KNOX, 1998, RECALLING THE *Princesses* ON THE TRIANGLE ROUTE EARLY IN THE SECOND WORLD WAR.

The *Princess Alice,* in wartime gray off Victoria's Ogden Point on August 18, 1945. –MAURICE CHANDLER

The *Princess Maquinna* continued throughout the war years on her traditional run to the West Coast of Vancouver Island. She is shown above at Victoria on August 23, 1945. –MAURICE CHANDLER

But problems with the non-CPR crew members supplied to the *Kathleen* and *Marguerite* were growing, with fights, drunkenness and other difficulties becoming serious. Finally on December 31, 1941, in despair, Capt. Leicester found a solution when they arrived in Ceylon (Sri Lanka). "I determined to get rid of the men... at all costs. To continue with such hooligans was practically out of the question.... The Company's *Empress of Russia* was in port and paying-off the Chinese Crew. I applied for and obtained a Crew from among those paid-off, obtaining permission from our London Office before doing so."

With the crew exchange, the situation improved instantly, and there was little trouble for the remainder of either ship's wartime service. From Alexandria on January 7, 1943, Capt. Barry reported to Capt. Douglas back in Victoria, that "we have escaped damage although we have had some tough assignments recently and morale is excellent. The engineers are a grand crowd of fellows and I could not wish for better."

Internal changes to the *Kathleen*, and to a lesser extent to the *Marguerite*, were extensive. Staterooms were retained on the boat deck for officers and staff but on the promenade deck, the smoking lounge became an officer's lounge and mess and all staterooms forward of the staircase were removed to clear large spaces for mess tables seating 560 and hammock space for 256. Below, on the lower deck, where once large suites and staterooms were situated, mess tables for 648 men were installed and 481 hammock spaces were cleared. Other staterooms gave way to a hospital, canteen and extra lavatories. The sitting room became in part a Sergeants' mess and a small dining saloon. Saltwater showers were added on the outside decks. The once gracious dining saloon was converted to more mess and hammock space for troops to seat 268 men and sleep 240. In total, the *Kathleen* was intended to provide mess seating for 1530 and hammock space for 1005 but this could be increased by 25 percent to 1255. In addition, cabin space was available for 107 officers.[46] Capt. Leicester commented, somewhat ruefully, in a voyage report, "As appears usual with embarkation authorities, when they find that 800 have been carried effectively, they are inclined to put 900 on board for the following occasion and then 1,000, and so on."[47]

Loss of the Marguerite, August 17, 1942

At 10:30 a.m. the *Princess Marguerite* sailed from Africa Basin, Port Said, Egypt, for Cyprus in convoy with three destroyers and the armed merchant cruiser *Antwerp*. The *Marguerite* was at the rear of the small convoy. After clearing the port and channel which was swept clear of mines, the convoy gathered speed and began a zig-zag course. Weather conditions were fine and clear with light westerly breezes. Between 1300 and 1330 the troops were

The *Princess Norah*, above, leaving Blubber Bay in August, 1943, and the *Princess Kathleen*, below, in the Mediterranean. –Edward Heppner photo, Peter Sawatsky collection; Capt. L. C. Barry, RBCM

Aflame from her pilot house to her stern, the stricken *Princess Marguerite* was doomed. –BC Archives, HP22744

There was the most horrific bang...

"I was sitting out on deck, talking to a British Soldier.... I told him there was nothing to worry about. There was the most horrific bang you ever heard. All safety valves blew and everybody scattered. I walked to my room, the door was burst open, on the port side. I got my life jacket and wallet and put it on and went around to my lifeboat on the other side and cleared it away. I didn't hear any word of abandoning ship from officers. We just did it on our own to lower the lifeboats. We lowered the lifeboat half way down to the promenade deck. The ship swung into the wind and fire swept down the deck. The guys manning the falls let my end go and my boat went down stern first into the drink with the Indian troops on top of each other. I fought my way free and started to swim out away from the ship. I looked up and I could see this destroyer coming over among us with scramble nets down, so I swam over there along with Tony Appleyard, the third mate. We scrambled up onto the destroyer. My right hand was very badly burned, with rope burns; I had a hold of the fall and it tore the skin off my hand. We were on the deck there with about 700 or 800 other men, and after we searched the wreckage and couldn't find anyone alive we headed back to Port Said. We buried about seven Indian troops who had died with oil in their lungs. Gave them a quick burial over the side..."

—Hugh Tumilty, Fifth Engineer, *Princess Marguerite*, recalling the sinking nearly 60 years later.

mustered for a boat drill and instructed on emergency procedures. Few on board guessed how important and timely it was.

"All went well until 1507, when a heavy explosion took place, shaking the ship violently from stem to stern, followed by the roar of escaping steam...." With these words Capt. Leicester began the report that detailed the loss of his beautiful ship.

"I went to the bridge immediately. Smoke was billowing out of the forward stokehold ventilators, and the accommodation on the Boat Deck abaft the Officer's quarters, this was followed by fire, which began to spread rapidly... throughout the ship....

"I at once gave the order to 'abandon ship,' the Officers passing my orders by word of mouth. The 4-inch gun was manned and trained in case opportunity for a shot should arise.

"Three of the boats on the port side were blown to pieces by the initial explosion, cabin doors were also blown off, and the longitudinal bulkheads on the upper decks... were also blown open, and fire raged throughout this accommodation from the stokeholds.

"At 1530 some fuel oil on the water alongside the port side of the ship took fire, making a considerable blaze stretching the length of the ship.

"Upon this, the Officers and crew hurried the remaining Troops over the starboard side in all manners possible (using fire hoses as ropes in some cases) telling them to strike out from the ship towards the destroyer...

"The ship was completely abandoned by 1545 and sank at 1556.

"Every praise is due the Troops for the way they behaved, there being no panic of any description.

"I am very proud of the behavior of my crew, both European and Chinese. They carried out their... duties under most trying conditions and I would say 90% of them swam for it. I wish particularly to bring to your notice the following:-

Edward Steward, 3rd Engineer.

William Harris, 6th Engineer.

...on duty in the Engineroom, for their presence of mind in carrying out their part of the drill in stopping the Main Engines. This was done in darkness all lights being out due to the auxiliary steam pipe being fractured, thus stopping all auxiliaries. The steam from this pipe was blowing across the upper part of the Engineroom at the forward bulkhead, and out through entrance to starboard side of same. Had the Engines not been stopped, there is no doubt that there would have been a very heavy loss of life.

Stanley Matthews, Electrician.

...for his part, in starting up the Emergency Dynamo, situated on the Boat Deck.

"Lives Lost: 5 Chinese crew, and approximately 50 Troops, out of a total of 1124 souls on board...."

–H. A. LEICESTER, MASTER. REPORT, *"Loss of ship due to enemy action"* August 17, 1942.

The survivors were picked up by the escorting vessels, in particular the destroyer HMS *Hero*, and fortunately, the water was warm. "You should have seen the men from the destroyer," recalled Bill Harris. "They had the best water polo team in the fleet and they went over the side like flies to rescue men from our ship." The Chinese crew was paid off at Alexandria, awaiting transport, and the British and Canadian crew members left Suez early in September on the troop ship *Oronsay* for the voyage to South Africa. Unfortunately, the British crew was transferred to the CPR liner *Duchess of Atholl* at Durban but she too was torpedoed en route to Britain on October 10, 1942. The Canadians sailed safely to New York. The fatal torpedo was fired by the German submarine *U-82* which itself was sunk by aircraft on March 4, 1943. Capt. Leicester retired from CPR service in 1955 as master of the *Empress of Scotland*, and died in 1967 at the age of 71. He and Chief Engineer William Neilson were awarded the O.B.E. for their valor during the sinking of the *Marguerite*. Engineers Edward Stewart and William Harris were awarded the M.B.E.[48]

The Kathleen's Wartime Diary

THE *Kathleen* WAS TO SPEND FOUR AND A HALF YEARS in the Mediterranean. Her duties were many and took her to dozens of ports. She carried Italian prisoners of war from Mesawa, Ethiopia, to Port Sudan in May 1942. She sailed into Tobruk on January 1, 1943 as the British Eighth Army pushed Rommel's Afrika Corps back towards the west. She was in Alexandria on September 16, 1943 when major units of the Italian fleet surrendered. On October 10, 1943, Capt. Barry and most of the Canadian crew were relieved and returned to Canada. Capt. Leonard Johnston, formerly of the *Empress of Asia*, took over and commanded the *Princess* for a year and 10 months. Shortly after the German surrender on May 8, 1945, "VE Day," she was at Rhodes and took on board as prisoners German General Wagner and his staff.

But winter had its hardships and the sea could be extremely rough. On a five-day voyage between Taranto, Italy, and Haifa, Palestine, between November 28 and December 3, 1944, 63 officers were carried in first class, 25 men in second class and 1,033 in third class. The voyage was uneventful except for rough weather and the officer commanding the troops reported:

"She simply vanished..."

"I was on HMS *Kelvin*, a destroyer, when a signal was received reporting the sighting of a submarine on the route being taken by a troopship named *Princess Marguerite*. She was ferrying troops from North Africa to Cyprus....We had been steaming all night at around 30 knots and shortly after dawn one of the lookouts on the bridge spotted the *Marguerite* and reported this to the Captain. I was one of the lookouts and as we trained our binoculars on the horizon we caught a last sight of her before she disappeared from view. We were too far away to hear the explosion nor did we see any flash. She simply vanished as though a conjurer had worked his magic. It was some two hours later and after we had ensured that the submarine was not still in the vicinity that we began picking up survivors. We picked up around 200 soldiers, none of whom I can remember as badly injured.... One soldier not only managed to find a piece of wreckage strong enough to support him but able to stand the weight of a crate of beer which quite clearly he had sampled in full. In contrast when we handed round some rum, some Indian soldiers, in line with their religious belief obeyed the Captain's injunction and heaved it over the side to the consternation of the ship's crew."

–THOMAS MALONE, GLASGOW, SCOTLAND, IN A 1985 LETTER TO BRYAN McGILL.

Condolences...

"We are all very sorry that this little *Princess* has gone as she was getting quite a name for herself in the way she got through to her destination and back again week after week." "However, like all coasters in this part of the world, sooner or later, 'they get it.' We have heard from several outside sources of the crew's splendid behavior when it came."

–W. T. BOND, PORT SAID & SUEZ COAL COMPANY, WHO HAD MADE ARRANGEMENTS FOR THE CREW, TO CANADIAN PACIFIC IN LONDON ON AUGUST 20.

Business-like and sombre, the *Princess Kathleen* awaits the next troop movements in support of the Allied Armies in the eastern Mediterranean.
–CAPT. L. C. BARRY, RBCM

"Slightly rough weather was encountered during this voyage and it has been almost impossible to keep to routine, due to the fact that approximately 50% of British Troops (4 Div. Adv. Party) and 95% of Cypriot Troops were down with sea sickness." The report noted that sanitary conditions were "consistent with abysmal sea sickness."

After VE Day, enemy action no longer threatened the *Kathleen* but her Mediterranean duties were far from over and some of the most stressful times were ahead. There were thousands of troops and displaced persons who needed transport. The *Kathleen* and her crew spent the next year running between such ports as Valetta, Tripoli, Taranto, Piraeus, Salonika, Bari, Port Said, Malta, Toulon, Haifa, Alexandria, Rhodes, Benghazi, Crete, Khios, Corfu, Patras, and on and on, criss-crossing the eastern Mediterranean, Adriatic and Aegean seas. Sometimes over 1600 people would be crowded aboard including British Army, Air Force or Merchant Navy personnel; Indian and Greek army troops; Greek, Yugoslav and Jewish refugees, some of whom were sick with tuberculosis and other illnesses; Italian prisoner of war families; German prisoners of war; and British civilians. Many people were frightened, disoriented, with few if any personal possessions, and not used to travel by sea. Others had so much baggage that it was extremely difficult to handle. There were chronic problems of language and translation, travel papers, lice, cleanliness and sanitation, providing adequate rations and drunkenness in some ports. Understandably there was often theft of bedding and other supplies. Some passengers were extremely co-operative, others were not. Standards, or at least caring, about cleanliness varied greatly. Some troops or refugees refused to do anything to assist in ship's maintenance, others left the ship clean and ready for the next voyage.

A voyage from Port Said in June 1945 could best be described as "the voyage from hell" for all aboard. Refugees embarked at Port Said included 250 men, 507 women and 607 children. Language difficulties, lack of interpreters and organization of the refugees before embarkation underlay many problems. And many, it seemed, had simply given up caring about anything in the aftermath of five or six years of war.

"There was a three hour delay before embarkation could commence owing to several sit down strikes, refusal to embark without their heavy baggage etc.," reported the *Kathleen*'s officer commanding troops at Alexandria. "Once on, they refused to sit at their mess tables during embarkation but wandered about and took up fresh positions on decks... making it impossible... to berth the remaining refugees. Within the space of a few hours the ship was in a filthy condition which became worse as time went on. A cleaning gang of 45 spent 3 days in Rhodes cleaning before the ship was fit to embark German PW." Fortunately, other voyages presented a contrasting picture, as the following note in a voyage report showed.

Conditions in the Mediterranean varied greatly. Summer brought heat and other problems....

"As a British soldier I boarded the *Princess Kathleen* in the Alexandria (Egypt) dock around the end of November, 1943, bound for Taranto and the Italian campaign. Contrary to popular belief, the Mediterranean can be extremely rough and, although very much over loaded, we were laying on the decks, exposed to the elements. *Kathleen*, bless her, rolled on back and forth to complete the journey safe and sound."

–ARCHIE H. J. SHONK, SOMERSET, UK, IN A 1985 LETTER TO BRYAN McGILL.

Medical Officer's Report...

Voyage Report
by Senior Medical Officer, S.S. *Princess Kathleen*.
Voyage Ending 15 Aug. 44

"1. The Medical health of the troops was good.
2. The cabins occupied by Permanent Staff and officers in transit are infested with bed bugs. In the Mess Decks the infestation is in the tables and benches and also in the hammocks. In the cabins it is in the beds and the woodwork of the bulkheads. The crew's quarters are also infested. The only method of eradication is fumigation with Cyanide.
3. The ship is swarming with cockroaches.

–HUBERT A. BLACKFORD, CAPT. RAMC
SENIOR MEDICAL OFFICER., S.S. *Princess Kathleen*."

Captain's report...

"The ship was fumigated with Cyanide Gas on May 14th of this year."

–CAPT. L. H. JOHNSTON, MASTER. 15TH. AUGUST 1944.

"The O.C's [officer commanding] and Medical Officer's reports do not adequately describe the stink and filth of this ship during the voyage and as left after disembarkation."

–CAPT. L. H. JOHNSTON, MASTER, *Princess Kathleen*.

Capt. Barry photographed an anti-aircraft gun crew on the *Kathleen* and also recorded his ship near Suez. The air photo shows the ship on a beautiful calm day. –CAPT. L. C. BARRY, RBCM

"Port Said/Split (Yugo-Slav Refugees)

No trouble experienced with these people, they keep their quarters clean and are very co-operative generally."

Finally, the *Kathleen's* transport service ended and in mid-1946 she headed home, 250,000 miles (over 400,000 km) of war time steaming behind her. In the last year and a half, she had steamed nearly 90,000 miles (145,000 km), called at 182 ports and carried nearly 100,000 people. Capt. Richard Leicester, brought the *Kathleen* back to Victoria. Capt. L. C. Barry, who had commanded the *Kathleen* for part of her service in the Mediterranean and who had become general superintendent of Canadian Pacific Steamships at Vancouver, was there to meet his old ship and friends. Capt. Leicester, who commanded the *Marguerite* and two other steamships, had taken over the *Kathleen* from Capt. Len Johnston late in 1945.[49]

By the end of the Second World War, the *Princess* fleet was in trouble and replacements were needed desperately. The *Vic, Charlotte, Alice, Adelaide, Mary* and *Maquinna* were all 35-40 years old and tired from the hard years of service from the war years. The *Marguerite*, lost in the war, would never return and the *Kathleen* needed extensive reconstruction. The rest of the fleet was at least 15 or 20 years old; no new boats had been built during either the Depression or the Second World War.

During the war years planning proceeded for new vessels for the Coast Service. Various alternatives were developed but it was clear that the Triangle Route and the Alaska service needed particular attention. Both were traditional services that had been lucrative. The aging steamers used in the Alaskan summer service were becoming increasingly inadequate and outdated. The construction of a new vessel suitable for cruises as well as relief on the Triangle Route was recommended in the 1930s but the Depression and the Second World War made new construction impractical. In the end, the solution was to build two new intercity steamers for the Triangle Route and refit the *Kathleen* for Alaska cruises and winter duties on the Triangle Route.

Shipyards were busy after the end of the war replacing tonnage and completing wartime orders. In 1943 the CPR reached an agreement with the Fairfield Shipbuilding & Engineering Company of Govan, Scotland, for the construction of two new steamers for the Coast Service as soon as berths became available. Specifications were finalized in 1945 but work did not begin immediately. Fairfield's first tenders were turned down by the CPR because of high costs but after revisions the contract was awarded on February 5, 1946. Eighteen percent of the costs of the new replacement for the *Princess Marguerite* were recovered from the British government's wartime tonnage replacement fund and further funds were payable from insurance accounts. These specified that vessels be built in Britain.

Meanwhile, the *Kathleen* returned to the Coast on August 1, 1946 and was extensively refitted at Esquimalt before returning to work on the Tri-City Route in May 1947 pending the arrival of the new steamers. The *Kathleen's* refit included a complete reconstruction of her passenger accommodations and a general overhaul and modernization. Despite the hard wartime service, mechanically she was still in excellent condition but the passenger accommodations had to be almost entirely renewed. She reappeared with simplified decor more in keeping with late 1940s styling but she was still elegant and a favourite on the Triangle Route.

The *Kathleen's* welcome addition to the intercity service permitted the withdrawal of the *Princess Alice*, weary from 36 years of almost constant service, and in need of extensive refitting if she were to continue in operation. Direct night boat service between Seattle and Vancouver resumed for the summer of 1947 and also ran in 1948 but after that it was never operated. Airlines, rail services and most of all improved highways took away the passengers. With the termination of the direct service between Seattle and Vancouver, the famed triangle of the Triangle Route was broken forever. Nonetheless, *Princess Lines* timetables continued to refer to the Triangle Route through the late 1950s.

An Old Friend Comes Home...

"There are ships and ships. Some of them mean nothing to anyone except those concerned with their doings. Others occupy a special place in the pride of a port and its citizens. The coastal steamers *Princess Kathleen* and *Princess Marguerite* were among the latter...

"They shared a popular attachment that is not wholly accounted for by their speed and palatial appointments. There was an indefinable link between them and the people of Vancouver and Victoria. Perhaps it was because they were the symbol of a better day. Whatever it was it will be nice to welcome the *Kitty* back home..."

–*Daily Province*, Vancouver, July 27, 1946.

After six long years, the Second World War ended and the *Princesses* entered a time of change and reconstruction. The *Princess Alice*, recorded in a classic CPR advertising photo, passed an idyllic vacation setting looking over the Oak Bay Golf Club near Victoria. The return to service of the *Princess Kathleen* after her reconstruction permitted the retirement of the *Alice*. The *Kathleen* was as beautiful as ever with her interior reflecting the simpler tastes of the post-war era. At right, in a fine portrait, she steams through the Gulf Islands on May 27, 1952. –Nicholas Morant, CP Archives; Canadian Pacific; and John Newman

The Maquinna and the Mary and the Coastal Routes

From Ahousaht to Nootka...

"I must have been about six years old. It was before I went to school, when I travelled with my aunt from Ahousaht to the cannery at Nootka. Many people from Ahousaht worked at the cannery in those days [the late 1940s and early 1950s]. At Ahousaht, we would meet the *Princess Maquinna* halfway out, coming out in small boats. We would get on through the freight doors on the side. When we got on, we didn't go upstairs right away. It was time to eat, so we dined first. The dining room was down in the hold. It was very simple, not elegant. Everyone ate together. There was a very large whiteman sitting at the table next to us. He had a big handkerchief and blew his nose very loudly, a big snort. My aunt shrieked, she was so startled. Everyone laughed.

"We really didn't have cultural eyes for things; we never really noticed, for example, the difference between fine china and cups that weren't fine. We were more aware of spiritual connotations—a different way of looking at the world. Later, I remember lying face down in my berth in the stateroom as we went around Estevan Point. Everything was creaking. I'd go up with the ship as it rose on the waves, and I'd be left behind in the air as it plunged. I don't recall leaving the ship at Nootka, so I may have been sleeping. They would have just packed me off in the night."

—Dr. Richard Atleo, Chief Umeek of Ahousaht, remembering travels on the *Princess Maquinna* as a young boy in the late 1940s.

The old ways of the coast were changing rapidly in the years after the Second World War and the steamships, once vital to everyone, were finding less and less traffic. The days when both the *Princess Mary* and *Princess Maquinna* docked at Bamfield below the cable station were passing. With the disappearing traffic went the capital needed for replacing the aging fleet. Aircraft increasingly took passengers away from the steamers, road connections were improving and there was little need to run the *Maquinna,* the *Norah,* or the other *Princesses* in passenger service along the exposed West Coast of Vancouver Island. Above, Quartermaster J. R. Dodge steers the *Princess Maquinna* on her West Coast route. —Vancouver Maritime Museum, left; and Dr. W. B. Chung collection

On the Powell River Route...

"My family always referred to the ship as "The Old Mary." I could never get 'close' to the *Mary*. For me it was a slow and uninteresting ship. I always felt that in terms of cleanliness it wasn't up to par with the ships that the CPR used on the Triangle Run.

"The *Mary* always seemed to depart Powell River for Vancouver at midnight. People would gather on the dock for 'good-byes' and wait until the last minute to board unless, of course, it was raining. Once all of the cargo was aboard, everyone would be advised to get aboard and then we would be off. When we awoke in the early morning, we would be tied up to the pier in Vancouver."

–KEN KNOX, 1998, RECALLING TRIPS TO POWELL RIVER BEFORE THE SECOND WORLD WAR.

The *Princess Mary's* service to Powell River and the Gulf Islands was being bypassed by highway development and car ferries and became an expensive albeit picturesque anomaly. In busier times, she is shown at right in port in Vancouver, with the *Princess Elaine* departing in the background. In the scene below the *Mary* is at Blubber Bay on Texada Island and to the right steaming through the First Narrows from Vancouver Harbour in May 1951.
–DR. W. B. CHUNG COLLECTION; VANCOUVER MARITIME MUSEUM; CLINTON BETZ

The Princesses in Transition

The Depression and the Second World War extended the lives of several of the aging *Princesses* but by the late 1940s, there was little that could be done, within reasonable economic expectations, to keep them running. The lovely *Princess Charlotte*, captured at left in a rare Kodachrome at Victoria, was relieved by the new *Princess Patricia* in 1949. She arrived at Victoria for the last time on June 14, that year. The *Princess Vic*, for so long the heart of the Coast Service, continued on to complete 47 years of service. These wonderful photos are a lasting reminder of these two fine old steamships.
–MAURICE CHANDLER, AUTHOR'S COLLECTION; JIM STEPHEN COLLECTION

The New Princesses: The Marguerite and Patricia

THE FIRST OF THE NEW STEAMERS WAS LAUNCHED on May 26, 1948 and named *Princess Marguerite* by Mrs. Robert McMurray, wife of the managing director of Canadian Pacific Steamships and formerly the manager of the B.C. Coast Steamship Service. Capt. McMurray brought the original *Marguerite* to British Columbia in 1925. The second vessel was launched on October 10, 1948 and was named *Princess Patricia* by Lady Patricia Ramsay, for whom, as the young Princess Patricia of Connaught, the first *Princess Patricia* had been named in 1912.

The new *Marguerite* ran her trials early in 1949 and sailed from the Clyde for Victoria on March 5, 1949. After a rough 9,600-mile (15,500-km) voyage she arrived at the quarantine station, at William Head near Victoria, on April 6, 1949. Welcoming receptions and a quick refitting at Esquimalt followed and the *Marguerite* made her first trip to Seattle on April 29, 1949. Two months later, on June 15, 1949, the *Princess Patricia* arrived in Victoria from Scotland and entered service soon after, permitting the well-deserved retirement of

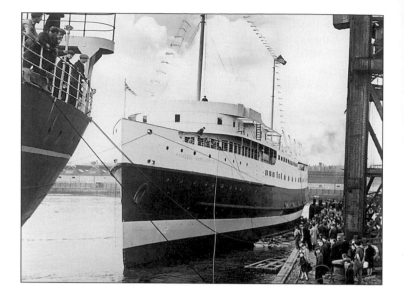

A new generation of *Princesses*, yet so familiar in appearance, came with the arrival of the *Princess Marguerite* and *Princess Patricia* in 1949. The upper photos show the *Marguerite* just after being launched on May 26, 1948 and in service at Seattle in August, 1955. The *Pat,* launched on October 6, 1948, was almost identical, but had her whistle mounted higher on the forward funnel.
–Canadian Pacific Archives; Roger M. Perry; and John Newman

Changes to the Triangle...

"With the introduction of the new *Princesses, Marguerite* and *Patricia,* the Triangle changed. What we did was dock one night in Nanaimo and the other night in Seattle. The day's run was from Nanaimo to Vancouver, [then to] Victoria and Seattle, and reverse it the next day from Seattle to Nanaimo."

–J. Gary Richardson, Steward.

The new Marguerite and Patricia...

"The successors of the *Marguerite* and *Kathleen,* the new *Marguerite* and *Patricia,* went into service in '49. Though very fine ships, they never, in my opinion, had the grandeur of their predecessors. Their passage ways and public rooms didn't have the hardwood flooring or carpets. Pale cold, composition floors (or decks) seemed to predominate. So did the coffee shop. The earlier ships did not, at the start of their careers anyway, have a coffee shop. Instead, a steward beating a gong or tapping the pipes announced the meal times. And what a meal for a dollar! What white Boston Clam Chowder!"

–Tom Goodlake, Purser.

Last Log Entries from the Princess Kathleen...

"2:58. Stop. Struck Pt. Lena
Emergency Alarm given immediately and life-boats swung out ready for lowering. Soundings taken and ship found to be taking water in fore peak. Soundings taken all around the ship.

"Engines manoeuvered in endeavor to pull the ship off the rocks. Wind steady and increasing to strong N. W.

"5:30 a.m. Ship began to list badly to port and the Master ordered all passengers to be put ashore. About 7:00 a.m. U.S. Coast Guard vessel came along side to assist in disembarking passengers.

"11:30 a.m. Master ordered all crew ashore.

"1:40 p.m. Ship slipped off the rock and sank by the stern."

–*Princess Kathleen's* Log, Trip 692, Sunday, September 7, 1952.

the *Princess Charlotte.* The *Charlotte,* the *Alice* and the *Adelaide,* each with four decades of service behind them, were sold to the Typaldas Brothers of Greece for use in the Mediterranean.

The *Marguerite* and the *Patricia* were, from most perspectives, prewar in design and concept, and were modernized versions of the *Princess Kathleen* and *Princess Marguerite* of 1925. Elegant, fast, and built to an evolving design that accommodated automobiles only with a grudging reluctance, they were at home with the earlier generations of their predecessors like the *Princess Victoria* and the *Charlotte.* It was true that they had postwar turbo-electric propulsion systems and fewer staterooms but those were the most significant concessions to modernity. Hardwood panelling, grand pianos, comfortable staterooms and spacious dining saloons were traditions of the BCCSS that a war and the coming prosperity of the 1950s could not banish from the *Marguerite* or the *Patricia,* at least not in their early years. They were coastal liners, not ferries, and the distinction was clear in every line and curve of their design: sharp, slightly raked, wave-cutting bows; twin funnels; cruiser sterns; tall masts; a speed of over 23 knots (26.5 miles or 42.5 km an hour); finely constructed and furnished cabins that were proportioned to complement the hull. The old *Princess Victoria,* dowager of the fleet, could have been proud of these third-generation *Princesses* for the Triangle Route. They were not the last *Princesses* built but they were the last of the long line of classically-designed steamships the CPR acquired for the B.C. Coast Steamship Service.

The new steamers were welcomed by travellers and were very popular but traffic did not warrant use of both all year long. From 1949 until 1953, during the winter months, the *Marguerite* ran a daytime service between Victoria and Vancouver and also made a Vancouver-to-Nanaimo trip in the evening, returning the next morning. Either the *Princess Joan* or *Princess Elizabeth* made a daytime, return trip between Victoria and Seattle. Subsequently, the *Princess Elaine* filled in on the winter service between Victoria and Vancouver and the *Marguerite* and *Patricia* were both laid up in Victoria.

Meanwhile, tragedy struck the beautiful *Princess Kathleen.* Near Juneau in the early morning hours of September 7, 1952, steaming at about 10 knots, she ran hard aground on Lena Point a mile and a half off course. Chief Officer C. W. Savage was in charge on the bridge at the time having relieved Capt. G.O. Hughes. The *Kathleen* grounded near the peak of the high tide and by morning her situation was very serious indeed. It proved impossible to work her free as the falling tide dropped her stern at an extreme angle. Capt. Hughes ordered the passengers ashore and as the tide rose on its inevitable cycle, the *Kathleen* flooded from the stern. By 11:30 that morning, the ship was doomed; two hours later the

Alaska Service Steamers

In the early 1950s, the Alaska service had been reduced to the *Princess Norah*, the refurbished *Princess Kathleen* and the *Princess Louise*. The *Kathleen* and the *Louise* were used in the summers on the cruise service while the *Norah* worked on freight and passenger services to the North Coast including Kitimat which was being developed as an aluminum smelting centre. At left, the *Norah* arrives at Skagway. On this page, the *Louise* and the *Yukon Princess*, the latter purchased to supplement the freighting capacity of the fleet, are at the White Pass dock at Skagway. – Dedman's Photo Shop

flooded stern pulled the bow free and she sank in 130 feet (40 m) of water. She had survived over four years of dangerous transport service in the Mediterranean, but this was the end. Salvage proved impractical for the *Princess Kathleen*. Fortunately, there was no loss of life and no one was injured of the 307 passengers and 119 crew aboard. The loss of the *Kathleen* was a terrible blow to the Coast Service, already suffering from a shortage of vessels and the *Kathleen* had always been more than just another vessel. She had been a symbol of the service; the ultimate *Princess*, and now, like the *Marguerite*, she was gone.

Once again, the *Princess Louise* became the primary vessel on the Alaska cruise service. But now, only the *Princess Norah* was available for North Coast service and additional capacity on the Alaska route.

Passing Ships and a Changing Coast

BUT LIFE ALONG THE COAST WAS CHANGING, and changing at a pace that few people could appreciate or anticipate. The resource-based communities were disappearing along with the canneries and logging camps that supported them. Declining fish stocks, changes in technology (in particular advances in cold storage) and economics encouraged a centralization of fish-processing industry in the major centres, particularly along the Fraser and Skeena rivers.

Road systems expanded on Vancouver Island and along the southern Mainland Coast; increasingly, people living in outlying communities could fly by float plane, amphibian or from regional airports instead of taking the long and sometimes frustratingly leisurely and now elderly coastal liners. Tug and barge services increasingly cut into freight revenues so important to the coastal liners. In the 1920s and 1930s there had been dozens of small communities, logging camps and seasonal canneries all along the coast dependent on steamships, but by the 1950s the numbers were dwindling rapidly and with them went the passengers, freight and mail that were the lifeblood of the steamship services. It wasn't just the CPR that felt the decline in traffic. Union Steamships and Canadian National Steamships also began to withdraw from the coastal trade. Underlining the shift in travel away from the steamers was the development and success of Queen Charlotte Airlines which, using a makeshift collection of rebuilt wartime amphibians and bush aircraft, was handling 85 percent of the passenger traffic to West Coast points with their aircraft seldom more than 40 percent full.

Another major addition to the fleet came in 1951 with the arrival of the largest *Princess* of them all in tonnage terms, the *Princess of Nanaimo*. Built at the Fairfield yards in Scotland and an impressive vessel, she was modern looking and well-built, but was in some

The Elizabeth Sailed North...

"That was the saddest day of my life when the *Kathleen* went down. I was a junior assistant purser on the *Elizabeth* at the time and we were at Nanaimo. The old man came down and asked for all crew to please assemble in the forward lounge before we took on passengers. We were told about the *Kathleen* and that we would go to top off our fuel bunkers, take on provisions and head up the coast immediately to pick up the passengers and crew off the *Kathleen*. We made all haste going north.

"At low tide just the tops of the masts of the *Kathleen* were showing. Salvage was considered too risky and expensive. It was a very sad time. She was the most beautiful ship to look at."

–PATRICK O. HIND, JUNIOR ASSISTANT PURSER.

When the Kathleen went down...

"When she was a little girl, our daughter Donna just loved the *Kathleen*. She loved them all but the *Kathleen* was her pride and joy and when that *Kathleen* sank, she said to Gran, "Gran, you know, this is the awfullest thing that has ever happened in my life or ever will have, except when Mummy and Daddy die!"

–PHYLLIS HORNE.

When the Maquinna died...

When she came to her end, she literally just sneezed real loud in Victoria harbour, and several tubes fell out of her boiler, and just like the famous one-horse shay, all came apart and she never sailed again after that night. She wasn't even able to sail to Vancouver. Every time she came in from that West Coast trip, during her turnaround time, she went from Victoria over to Vancouver on a non-passenger freight run, and then came back and picked up her passengers. She'd been over to Vancouver, had come back to Victoria, and when she got ready to sail from Victoria, they just couldn't steam her. She was losing more water than they could put in. And I have often thought, 'What the hell would have happened to us, if she had come apart that night when we were steaming along off Estevan Point?' Now I've been at sea in some pretty bad weather, but I think that was one of the worst passages I've ever made with the wind blowing like that, and the seas so steep, and I think the reason they were steep was because we were so close to shore. Up there, you know, those waves come all the way from Russia. There's nothing to stop them. And then all of a sudden they're shallowing up...."

—Commodore Lester G. Arellanes, in 1990 recalling the *Maquinna* shortly before her retirement.

After nearly 50 years, the Princess Vic was retired...

"Later in the season [1950] the Union went on strike.... We stayed at anchor in Vancouver about three days when we got news that the *Princess Victoria* was to be scrapped. So I made the last trip of any steward in the dining room all by myself.... I spent the rest of this summer just going to work eight hours a day. Each morning I would start and just do simple things like taking the sheets off the beds, and then the toilet paper out of the staterooms. We took the carpets and mattresses out. On and on it went until we had gutted the ship. We went into the dining room and every dish and piece of silver was taken out and we ended up in the galley where we took out all the pots and pans that the Chinese cooks had used. This is a special memory."

—J. Gary Richardson, BCCSS Steward.

The Princess Mary, after 40 years and changing times...

Newspapers called her "outdated, outpaced, outworn," and indeed she was. Some even called her an "old tub," sometimes with affection, sometimes without. Except for the wear and tear of 40 years, the *Mary* had changed little from the boat once called lavish and luxurious; only the people had, and their expectations and needs.

Fraser Bruce provided a tribute to the *Mary* in Victoria's *Daily Colonist* in 1952. "Her visits regulated the social life of the [Gulf] islands. Boat days brought the inhabitants out in force to stare at the passengers and be stared at in turn; to watch the crew restoring to anxious parents a small traveller who had made the passage 'alone,' soothing a cow who resented her airborne delivery, unloading freight ranging from teacups to tractors. Meanwhile, the children swarmed up the ship to buy ice cream, and last-minute letter-writers popped their mail into the convenient box at the gangway."

ways obsolete by the time she was placed in service. With an automobile capacity of 140 cars, the *Nanaimo* was still designed for side loading and unloading. The *Nanaimo* was intended to replace the 23-year-old *Princess Elaine* as the primary vessel on the Nanaimo–Vancouver route and was the last *Princess* built with a steam propulsion system.

A tragic fire on the Canada Steamship Lines' cruise steamer *Noronic* in 1949 while berthed in Toronto harbour, resulted in much stricter regulations for fire protection for vessels and in particular those with wooden cabins. The older *Princesses* and the *Motor Princess* had wooden cabins and could not be economically modernized. The *Vic,* nearing 50 years of service, was worn out and her wooden cabins no longer met these new standards. The *Mary,* at over 40 years of age, and with repairs of nearly $625,000 needed to refit her, was retired in 1951 with some of her cabins becoming the Princess Mary Restaurant in Victoria. The *Maquinna,* whose boiler failed at Victoria, soon followed her running mates into retirement and was replaced temporarily by the Frank Waterhouse Co. freighter *Chilliwack* and later the Union Steamship's *Veta C.* In 1953 the CPR purchased the freighter *Pomare,* renamed it the *Princess of Alberni,* and continued a freight service until 1958. All three veteran *Princesses* were scrapped with their hulls being used as barges. The *Motor Princess* also was withdrawn from passenger service and the summertime route between Steveston and Sidney was abandoned. But instead of scrapping, the *Motor Princess* got a reprieve and was used in freight service between Victoria and Vancouver until late 1953 when, in need of extensive refitting to her cabins and engines, she was retired. The reliable *Princess Joan* and *Princess Elizabeth* were modified to carry more freight to compensate for the removal of the *Motor Princess* from freight duties.

The pending retirement of the *Mary* and the *Maquinna* came as no surprise to anyone in the Coast Service. Both steamers still had their original engines and boilers, their reliability was highly questionable and officials knew that their certificates would not be renewed. They were obsolete in design and were not suited to the services needed in the 1950s. The *Mary,* which could carry only a few automobiles, reflected the needs of earlier generations, not those of the 1950s. The West Coast route could not justify the costs of new construction but Capt. Williams, the Coast Service manager, felt a new vessel could be made to pay, at least if a subsidy were offered, on the *Mary's* route to the Gulf Islands and to Powell River. However, while a replacement for the *Mary* was under consideration, the entire question was made irrelevant when Capt. Alexander Peabody's Puget Sound Navigation Company transferred the small automobile ferries *Bainbridge* and *Quillayute,* no longer needed in Washington, to Canadian registry and established a service that linked Powell River with Vancouver via road and two short ferry trips. Any remaining business on the Powell River

Triangle Route Finale

The 1950s was the last decade of full service on the Triangle Route, although the direct Seattle–Vancouver night boats no longer operated. For travellers, it was an opportunity to ride on the new *Marguerite* and *Patricia* or the now elderly *Princess Joan* or *Princess Elizabeth*. Even the *Princess Elaine* strayed from her primary service between Vancouver and Nanaimo to work the day time service between Vancouver and Victoria. This selection of colour photos captures these *Princesses* in those last years before the advent of the B.C. Ferries system and the withdrawal of the coastal liners from nearly all of their traditional services. At left, the *Princess Elizabeth* berthed in Victoria in beautiful summer weather in the early 1950s and above, the *Princess Joan* in drydock at Esquimalt. The *Princess Marguerite* steams through the First Narrows at Vancouver and the *Elaine* churns through Active Pass on a beautiful July 29, 1954. –ALBERT TURNER; AND MAURICE CHANDLER, THREE PHOTOGRAPHS, AUTHOR'S COLLECTION

route disappeared. The CPR finally modified the *Princess Elaine* as a stopgap measure for the Gulf Islands route but she was not well suited to the small ports and passages and could be employed more effectively on the Nanaimo route. Nonetheless, residents of the Gulf Islands needed improved ferry services and this was provided by the Gulf Islands Ferry Company (1951) Ltd., whose president was Gavin Mouat from Saltspring Island. The company operated the little ferry *Cy Peck*, formerly the *Island Princess*, between Fulford Harbour on Saltspring Island and Swartz Bay a few miles north of Sidney. They purchased the *Motor Princess* in January 1955 for reconstruction as an open-decked automobile ferry and began service in June 1956 between Swartz Bay and the southern Gulf Islands. The *Princess Elaine* returned to the services for which it was intended and the *Motor Princess* was eventually to be incorporated into B.C. Ferries as the *Pender Queen*.[50]

While the population of the isolated coastal communities was dwindling, urban centres and larger towns with good road access were prospering. More and more people were purchasing cars and wanting to travel with them. The stately *Princesses*, with the exception of the new *Princess of Nanaimo*, the dumpy little *Motor Princess,* the *Princess Elaine* and the reconstructed *Princess Victoria,* were not designed primarily with cars in mind. Even on the newer vessels, the loading was slow and cumbersome. At the same time, new or substantially remodelled automobile ferries were entering service on Puget Sound and the very modern *Chinook* was running to Victoria.

A damaging blow to the Coast Service came in 1953 when Black Ball Ferries, a Canadian subsidiary of Washington's Puget Sound Navigation Company, began a fast and frequent automobile ferry service between Horseshoe Bay, near West Vancouver, and Departure Bay just north of Nanaimo on Vancouver Island. Black Ball used the rebuilt ferry *Kahloke*, which was soon supplemented by the much newer *Chinook,* running as the *Chinook II*. These plain, functional vessels hardly seemed competition for the *Princesses* but they were, and their threat was mortal. The fast, no-frills service was efficient and designed for rapid loading and unloading of vehicles. No reservations were offered, vehicles were packed in and costs were minimized.

The prosperity of the 1950s was no longer reflected in the balance sheets of the Coast Service. By the mid-1950s, the CPR was facing a deadly serious battle for this growing trade but its fleet was poorly equipped for this type of service. It was the beginning of the end for the B.C. Coast Steamship Service and a time of retrenchment. The company focused almost entirely on the Seattle–Victoria–Vancouver route, the Victoria–Vancouver night boats, the Nanaimo–Vancouver automobile ferry run and the summertime Alaska cruise service. Although the CPR studied the possibilities of building new automobile ferries and devel-

Service to the Gulf Islands faded in the 1950s and was replaced by automobile ferries. These photos show the *Motor Princess* at Galiano Island and the *Princess Norah* at Mayne Island, in the late 1930s, with a seat commemorating the coronation of King George VI in the foreground. –DONALD A. NEW PHOTO AT TOP, BOTH AUTHOR'S COLLECTION

The *Princess of Vancouver*, a motor vessel, was the last major addition to the fleet during the 1950s. She was designed to carry railcars, automobiles and passengers and largely replaced the tug and railway barge service to Vancouver Island. On her delivery voyage from Scotland she carried a cargo of English cars. Their small size illustrates a dilemma that faced the ferry operators. Vehicles during the 1950s and 1960s increased greatly in size making the deck spaces on the ships increasingly cramped and reducing economic returns. –DAVID SCHOLES; CANADIAN PACIFIC

oping a more efficient vehicle-oriented service by relocating its terminals to possible sites between White Rock and Horseshoe Bay, no action was taken. With revenues down and many demands on capital for postwar modernization, investment in the steamship service was no longer an inviting option. The window of opportunity had slipped by and the Coast Service would never again regain the initiative. Its place as the dominant shipping presence on the coast was fading.

The one exception to the decline in the service was the construction of the last major passenger-carrying *Princess*, the *Princess of Vancouver*, built at the A. Stephen & Sons yard in Glasgow, and placed in service in 1955. The new *Princess* was built not so much to counter Black Ball as it was to solve another looming problem for the Coast Service. The fleet of tugs and railcar barges serving Vancouver Island was operating at a loss, yet reinvestment in transfer barges was needed. Of the CPR tugs used on the barge service to Vancouver Island, only the *Kyuquot* remained in service and the Coast Service had to rely on expensive charter arrangements to move railway barges to Vancouver Island.

The *Princess of Vancouver*, an unusual stern-loading vessel similar to the multi-purpose vessels in use on the Great Lakes, was intended to carry passengers, automobiles and trucks as well as railway cars. Initially, her capacity was 28, 40-foot railcars, 110-120 automobiles or, as often happened, a combination of both. Drivers could find themselves squeezing their Chevys, Fords and Austins between 40-foot freight cars on the *Vancouver's* car deck. Diesel-powered, the new *Princess* featured a bow-mounted propeller for easier docking. The CPR also built a new railway transfer slip and pier west of Pier B-C in Vancouver as well as a new combined ferry slip and transfer wharf at Nanaimo where new waterfront rail yards were established for the Esquimalt & Nanaimo Railway. At 5,554 gross tons, the *Vancouver* was an impressive vessel but her multi-function design meant that she could be slow at terminals and only three return trips each 24 hours were scheduled for her on the Vancouver–Nanaimo route. In contrast, Black Ball was operating both of its cheaper vessels on five return trips a day between Horseshoe Bay and Departure Bay.

By the mid-1950s only the *Princess Norah* remained on the old coastal trade routes to the north coast and the makeshift *Princess of Alberni*, a replacement for the *Maquinna*, provided a residual freight service to the West Coast of Vancouver Island. In 1955, the CPR and Canadian National reached an agreement for the joint operation of the *Princess Norah* to north coast ports and she was renamed the *Queen of the North*.

The low point for the B.C. Coast Steamship Service came in 1958 when the entire fleet was hit by a lengthy strike by the Seamen's International Union. Eventually Black Ball was paralyzed when the Canadian Merchant Service Guild and the National Association of

The Vancouver-Nanaimo Service

The late 1940s through the early 1960s were the last years of steamship service on the Vancouver to Nanaimo route. Here, the *Princess Joan* passes the freighter *Thorshall* under the Lions Gate Bridge on September 9, 1957. Below, she is shown under the Greek flag as the *Hermes*. At Nanaimo, a newly refurbished *Princess Kathleen* was at the modernized passenger and car terminal about 1950. Below left, the *Princess Elaine* at Pier B-C. The post-war generation of vessels for the Vancouver–Nanaimo route, at right, was a major reinvestment by the CPR. The upper photo shows the *Princess of Nanaimo* at Pier B-C, while at right she steams under the Lions Gate Bridge on February 9, 1954. The *Kyuquot* was the last CPR steam tug in service and was sold in 1962. The *Princess of Vancouver* eases up to her ferry slip in fog at Vancouver on November 19, 1972. —Maurice Chandler; Jack Lenfesty; and, two photos below, Jim Stephen collection; at right, Victor Lomas photo, Royal B.C. Museum; Maurice Chandler two photos; and Robert D. Turner

Marine Engineers also went on strike. The net result was the creation of the government-owned B.C. Ferries Corporation and the almost complete withdrawal of the CPR from coastal services in British Columbia and Washington.

The *Queen of the North*, the former *Princess Norah,* and the *Princess of Alberni* were sold in 1958 to Northland Navigation. Under Northland's flag, the *Norah* became the *Canadian Prince.* Northland, a few local operators of smaller vessels and tug and barge companies provided the last shipping services, except for the modern ferry fleets, along the B.C. coast.

The night boats were withdrawn in February 1959 ending as well the Victoria–Seattle daytime service. Soon the *Joan* and the *Elizabeth* were sold to a Greek shipping line. The *Marguerite* provided a day service between Victoria and Vancouver until that summer when, joined by the *Patricia*, they both operated on the Tri-City service. The *Elaine* ran on the Victoria–Vancouver service for the winter months.

In June 1960 the new British Columbia Ferries vessels came into service providing a sailing every two hours in each direction, from 7:00 a.m. to 9:00 p.m., between Swartz Bay, north of Victoria, and Tsawwassen, south of Vancouver. The *Marguerite* and *Patricia* ran that summer as usual on the Tri-City route but at the end of the summer the service was cancelled as was the winter day service between Vancouver and Victoria. Fast, easy to load automobile ferries had won over the traditionally-designed *Princesses* and Vancouver–Victoria service would never be reinstated by the CPR, but the *Marguerite* provided a summertime service between Seattle and Victoria with an additional return trip to Port Angeles from Victoria.

In the summer of 1962, the *Patricia* and *Marguerite* ran to Seattle because of the popular World's Fair. However, that summer was just a brief time of renewed activity. At the end of the season, the *Marguerite* and *Patricia* were laid up in Victoria, the *Princess of Nanaimo* and the *Princess Elaine* were both withdrawn from the Nanaimo–Vancouver route and the *Louise* was retired from Alaska cruise service. Only the *Princess of Vancouver* remained in service that winter. Thereafter, the *Princess Marguerite* stayed on the summer-only Seattle–Victoria service, the route that was to become so intimately associated with the coastal liner, and she also made trips to Port Angeles from Victoria. The *Princess Patricia* was refitted for the Alaska cruise trade, replacing the *Princess Louise.* The three remaining *Princesses* were augmented by truck ferries but passenger services were clearly in their twilight years. The *Vancouver* was rebuilt internally to increase her vehicle capacity in 1962 and similar modifications were made to the *Marguerite* in 1972-73.

A diversion came for the *Pat* in the winters of 1965-66 and 1966-67 when she was chartered to operate between Los Angeles and Acapulco by Princess Cruises. These leisurely

Skagway Memories...

"It was always a treat to go on board the *Princess Pat* with our mother and it made my brother and me feel very important. I was probably seven and he about nine. We'd get to visit our friends Kathy, who ran the gift shop, and Ernie who was the Chief Steward. The gift shop was tiny but we also got to sit in the dining room and have sodas.

"One time in the early 1950s, my grandmother, Barbara Kalen, and her four children were fishing right outside the harbour and a storm came up so quick she couldn't row in in time. They were blown up against the *Princess Norah* and were rescued soaking wet onto the lower deck."

– AVERILL HARP, PROPRIETOR OF DEDMAN'S PHOTO & GIFT SHOP IN SKAGWAY.

The business was founded in 1924 by Bessie Dedman at the same location as E. G. Hegg's photo studio founded in 1898. Subsequently her daughter Barbara Kalen ran the business before her daughter Averill Harp took over management. The Dedman studio produced many fine photos of the *Princesses* and the White Pass & Yukon and several are reproduced in this book.

The *Princess Patricia*, at Skagway in September 1978. –ROBERT D. TURNER

The *Princess of Vancouver* leaving Burrard Inlet in 1973 on her way to Nanaimo on one of her three daily trips to Vancouver Island. –ROBERT D. TURNER

The *Carrier Princess*, shown at Nanaimo in 1974, was the last new vessel built for the B.C. Coast Service, and although built as a truck and railcar carrier, it did have limited passenger accommodations. Briefly, a passenger service was operated between Swartz Bay and Vancouver. –ROBERT D. TURNER

With flags flying, the *Princess Marguerite* backs into Elliott Bay on September 30, 1974 for her last sailing as a Canadian Pacific vessel. –CLINTON BETZ

trips marked the beginning of the very successful operations of this company. The *Pat*, designed for northern waters, was not suited to the hot weather conditions of Mexican waters and new vessels were soon acquired for the lucrative cruising market.

On September 30, 1974, the CPR retired the *Princess Marguerite*, losses having mounted to $272,000 in the previous three years.[51] But fortunately for the *Marguerite*, more years of service lay ahead and that story unfolds in the next chapter. Only the *Princess of Vancouver* remained in the CPR's intercity passenger service although briefly the new *Carrier Princess*, designed primarily as a truck and railcar ferry, did carry passengers between Swartz Bay and Vancouver. The *Vancouver* was retired by the CPR on May 30, 1981, and was then sold to the British Columbia Ministry of Highways for use on its Powell River to Comox route. Modified by Highways, the *Vancouver* became a bow-loading vessel following shipyard surgery that, while improving her functionality, certainly did little for her lines. The *Patricia*'s service on the Alaska cruises also ended in 1981 and she was retired that fall at the end of the season. For the CPR, over 80 years of passenger steamship services on the Washington, British Columbia and Alaska coasts was at an end.

The Lovely, Lamented
Princess Marguerite

❧

"When we went on the **Princess Marguerite** *to see the King Tut Exhibit in Seattle, it was like going back 50 years with the beautiful wooden panelling and the dining room with linen table cloths, and a waiter serving you at the table. It was very special and a lovely experience...."*

—PETER CORLEY-SMITH.

"When the **Princess Marguerite** *sailed from Seattle for the last time, people cried...."*

—LORNE CAMPBELL, B.C. STEAMSHIP COMPANY AT SEATTLE.

The *Princess Marguerite*, at left, returned to service in the spring of 1975 in a striking white colour scheme. Meanwhile, the *Princess Patricia*, below, continued on the Alaska cruise service. —ROBERT D. TURNER; MAURICE CHANDLER

CHAPTER 4

The Marguerite & the Seattle Service, 1975–1989

THE FINAL CHAPTER IN THE STORY OF THE *Princess* COASTAL LINERS is really the story of the *Princess Marguerite's* last decade on the Seattle–Victoria route. After this service was cancelled by the CPR in 1974, the *Marguerite* was offered for sale but although there were interested groups associated with regional tourism, they could not raise the necessary funding to purchase and operate the vessel. Finally, on April 1, 1975, the *Marguerite* was sold to the Province of British Columbia.

The province paid $2,475,000 for the *Marguerite* and 8.7 acres (3.5 ha) of waterfront property along the south side of Victoria's Inner Harbour. Also included in the sale was the Rattenbury-designed Coast Service terminal building, which by that time was being used to house a wax museum. The ship itself represented $275,000 of the total transaction. Shortly after, a new provincially-owned Crown corporation, the British Columbia Steamship Company (1975) Ltd., became the successor to the CPR's 70-year tradition of operating steamships between Seattle and Victoria. Harry Tyson, who had retired as manager of marine operations for the Coast Service on September 1, 1973, resumed his responsibility for the *Marguerite* as general manager with the new company. Hugh Tumilty, superintendent engineer with the Coast Service, oversaw the ship's refit.

In 1972, the automobile capacity of the *Marguerite* had been increased by the conversion of passenger spaces into expanded car decks providing room for an additional 30 cars. Although effective in meeting the demand for vehicle traffic, these renovations only made the remaining passenger lounges more crowded and did little for the image of elegance and luxury that were key features in the *Marguerite's* original popularity and attractiveness for tourists.

The *Marguerite* needed an extensive refit before returning to service that spring. The work was carried out at Burrard Dry Dock in North Vancouver. Internal modifications expanded her lounge spaces, added a day-care area and much more seating, refurbished and enlarged her dining room, reopened the coffee bar, refurbished the bar and lounge, added a new cocktail lounge, and converted the upper car deck, recently rebuilt from staterooms, into a spacious lounge. Overall, the refitting cost $1.1 million. The *Marguerite's* facelift included a new, tourist-oriented image that featured a white hull and stylized Union Jacks on the funnels and stern. Intended to appeal to tourists from the United States, the merits of the design as an aesthetic and publicity notion were subject to considerable debate and diversity of opinion, ranging from dreadful to attractive, but whatever the conclusion the design was to stay with the ship for the rest of her career. On the internal modifications, however, the opinion was unanimous: the *Marguerite* was substantially improved and much more attractive for travellers.[53]

Initially, docking facilities at Seattle were a concern because the elevator at Pier 64 needed work but for $25,000 this too was repaired, so that the *Marguerite* could load about 50 or 55 vehicles on her car deck.

Following inaugural cruises on May 31 and June 1, 1975, the *Marguerite* re-entered passenger service, providing a return trip from Seattle to Victoria and a return sailing to Port Angeles during the afternoon. The Seattle to Victoria voyage was scheduled to take four hours with the basic fare set at $10 per passenger for a one-way trip with round trip excursion fares of $14 and a one-way automobile fee of $10. Capt. George C. Black was recruited from recent retirement to return to the *Marguerite* and Capt. Douglas Adlem, formerly of Canadian National's *Prince George*, was the relief captain. Walter Phillips was chief engineer. Many other former CPR employees returned to work on the *Marguerite*.

The *Marguerite*, in her new career, was ever a political creature. She was saved by the New Democratic Party government led by Premier Dave Barrett and overseen by his resources minister Robert Williams; the Barrett government had little support in the business community yet the *Marguerite* project was intended to help support the tourism industry. An 18-member advisory committee was appointed to help and although it included people from many political perspectives it did not remove the *Marguerite* from politics. The government saw the steamship service as key to enhancing the tourist industry in Victoria and felt that any losses in operations—although publicly at least it projected profitability— would be offset by the economic benefits to the economy of the Victoria region.[54] By late June, Robert Williams announced that the *Marguerite* was operating on a break-even basis even before the peak traffic season was fully underway. Certainly the public response was positive and the ship was often running near capacity.

Seeing potential in developing the service further with the possibilities of cruises, the B.C. Steamship Company also acquired the recently retired Canadian National Steamship's *Prince George*. However, before the 1976 season began, a change of government had come to British Columbia. For the new Social Credit administration of Bill Bennett, the *Marguerite*, of whose purchase and administration the Socreds had been highly critical, was no longer a favoured project but rather one that was simply tolerated. The *Prince George* was sold and in 1976 the *Marguerite's* Port Angeles service was cancelled.

The Marguerite's Manager, Harry Tyson...

"The government couldn't have picked a better guy for the job if they tried.... He brings to the job a wealth of experience and expertise plus a vast love for Victoria and surroundings and maybe a million and a half friends. One would have to say that if anybody can make a success out of running the Seattle ferry it would be Harry Tyson.

–JOHN MACKIN, COMMENTARY ON VICTORIA RADIO STATION CKDA, APRIL 11, 1975.

Harry Tyson returned from retirement to manage the *Marguerite's* operations in 1975. He had worked with the CPR for 49 years and seen the Coast Service through the difficult years of declining traffic to build the fleet of truck and railcar ferries that outlasted all of the coastal liners. Harry Tyson retired again in 1975 and was succeeded, before the sale to Stena, by Robert McHaffie, Arthur Elworthy, David Price, Barry Margetts and Ed Lien. –CANADIAN PACIFIC

The *Marguerite* at Seattle's Pier 69 with a large crowd of travellers waiting to board the steamer in 1981. –ROBERT D. TURNER

Oh, those flags...

"When the *Princess Marguerite* sails into Victoria for the first time this summer, adorned in her new color scheme, there will be a lot of people who won't know whether to laugh, cry or blow up....

"The funnels, no longer the traditional buff and black of the previous owner [actually more recently red and white] will be ablaze with red, white and blue in the design of the crosses that make up the British Flag. Around the stern, highlighting the all-white hull and natural wood deck-work will be another Union Jack - not the complete Jack, but half of it.

"As for the rest of the ship, the designers have done a skillful job of proposed remodelling...."

–MAURY GWYNNE, *The Victorian,* APRIL 23, 1975.

With the acquisition of the *Vancouver Island Princess*, the B.C. Steamship Company started sailings from Ogden Point where cars could be handled more readily. The *Marguerite* continued to sail into Victoria's Inner Harbour.
–ROBERT D. TURNER

By the end of the 1979 season, the *Marguerite* was due for refitting and the government announced she was to be retired. Protests to the contrary, the decision remained firm but the government did plan to transfer the *Queen of Prince Rupert* from the B.C. Ferries' fleet to the Seattle–Victoria service. However, because of her lack of side-loading doors, no cars were to be carried and, to supplement the ferry, which was smaller than the *Marguerite*, a Boeing hydrofoil called the *Flying Princess* was leased to augment the service. Renamed the *Victoria Princess*, the *Rupert* made two return trips a day to Seattle but the service lost money and was not popular. The point that was missed was that the *Marguerite* herself was the major attraction. The second trip of the day soon was cancelled and by the end of the summer it was very clear that things had not worked out well. The *Rupert* returned to B.C. Ferries operations, the *Flying Princess* quietly disappeared and the *Marguerite* was refitted.

The investment in the *Marguerite* was significant and if the government had been a reluctant owner of the steamship, it did an about face and carried out a thorough refit. In fact the costs of refurbishing her machinery, making necessary repairs, adding retention tanks for the sanitary systems, renovating her lounges, and making much needed improvements to food preparation areas, which had received only minimal attention in her 1975 refit, came to an estimated $4.7 million, reflecting both the extent of the work and mid-1970s inflation. And so in late spring 1981, the *Princess Marguerite,* often affectionately called the *Maggie,* returned to the Seattle–Victoria service that she knew so well.

The 1980s were good years for the *Marguerite*. Her Seattle–Victoria schedule was leisurely and from late spring until late summer or early fall each year she carried thousands of visitors to and from Victoria. In 1987, the *Princess of Vancouver*, no longer needed by the B.C. Ministry of Highways, was transferred to the B.C. Steamship Company and renamed the *Vancouver Island Princess*. The big ferry was refitted at a cost of $2.3 million, including the replacement of her bow, for the Seattle service.

But the *Princesses* were not to live happily ever after and their reprieve proved all too short. In 1988, the government of Premier Bill Vander Zalm, Bill Bennett's successor as leader of the Socreds, announced plans for the privatization of the Seattle–Victoria service and the sale of the *Princess Marguerite* and *Vancouver Island Princess*. The European-based Stena Line purchased a 90 percent share of the operation in November for $6 million, creating the B.C. Stena Line.[55] The *Marguerite*, now featuring gambling aboard as a source of revenue, operated for only one more year and did not carry automobiles that season. She was retired on just three days' notice at the end of the 1989 season. Stena's most obvious contribution to the *Marguerite* was the garishly-painted "STENA LINE" that was applied to her hull and the *Vancouver Island Princess* received similar decoration.

From the start the Stena operations were controversial and trouble-plagued. In November 1989 Stena refitted a promised new vessel in Germany rather than in B.C. as originally announced. The next year Stena brought out from Europe the massive ferry *Crown Princess Victoria*, with its on-board gambling facilities which had been authorized by the B.C. government as an enticement for Stena to take over the service. Then, because the new vessel was of foreign registry, Stena faced pilotage fees in Washington of $1.8 million, which, with some last minute negotiations, were avoided. New services to Vancouver and Port Angeles from Victoria were proposed then dropped. After retiring the *Marguerite*, all Victoria Stena sailings were from Ogden Point and they planned an overnight sailing between Victoria and Seattle and operation of the new vessel on an all-year basis.[56]

Meanwhile a new company, Clipper Navigation, established a fast catamaran ferry service for passengers between Seattle and Victoria. The small high-speed craft proved popular and profitable and a formidable adversary for Stena. Clipper also questioned the length of time gambling was permitted on the Stena vessels and won an injunction to reduce the time to just 30 minutes.

The *Crown Princess Victoria* was not successful on the Seattle service and ran only during that summer, amid rumors of high losses and the Internal Revenue Service threatening $2,000,000 in back taxes. The *Vancouver Island Princess*, unofficially often called the *VIP*, also operated in the summer of 1990 at a loss, making her last sailing on November 15, 1990. The next month, B.C. Stena returned the larger vessel to its parent company along with supplies and materials from the *Princess Marguerite* and on November 13, 1990, Stena announced the closing of its Victoria-based operations. The loss of the service, which carried more than 300,000 people a year to Victoria, was estimated to cost the local economy as much as $75 million a year.[57] On November 15, Victoria's *Times-Colonist's* lead story by Les Leyne opened with a lucid summary of government reaction: "The privatization operation was a success–despite the death of the patient. That seemed to be the dominant Socred cabinet view... in the wake of B.C. Stena's shutdown...."

The collapse of the Stena Line operations in B.C. and Washington was the kiss of death for the *Marguerite*. Offered for sale in the fall of 1989 for $1.57 million US, although carried with a nominal book value of just one dollar, the *Marguerite* remained idle in Esquimalt until she was finally sold in November 1991 to Sea Containers Ltd. of Great Britain. She was towed out of Victoria for Singapore on February 20, 1992. Amid plans and promises of being rebuilt with diesel engines for continued service, then as a floating hotel in Southeast Asia, the *Marguerite* was never to operate again; she was sold, then scrapped in India in 1996.

Three generations enjoy breakfast in the *Princess Marguerite* dining saloon in 1981: Isabella Turner, who remembered the war years on the *Princesses* and the young servicemen who would never return home; Molly Turner, whose memories would be faint childhood recollections; and Nancy Turner, whose family came to Vancouver Island in the 1950s, and who, growing up in Victoria, remembered the *Princesses* as an everyday feature of Victoria's waterfront. –ROBERT D. TURNER

The *Marguerite* filled Seattle's Ballard Locks on the way to Lake Union on a special cruise in April 1983. –JOHN RITCHIE PHOTO, WARREN WING COLLECTION

Last Voyages

"I'll miss her soul. This ship is so alive. She really is. And she knows its her last day."

— Starmen Michael, Purser on the *Marguerite*, interviewed by Ed Watson for CBC Television on September 17, 1989.

They were sad days in Seattle and Victoria when the *Princess Marguerite* and *Vancouver Island Princess* made their final sailings. The *Marguerite* left Seattle for the last time on September 18, 1989 and the *VIP* ended her service on November 15, 1990. —Robert D. Turner

There were many proposals for operating the *Marguerite* in some way; some were little more than wishful thinking while others were serious and carefully thought out plans. None, however, could find the necessary financial backing or sufficient civic support. For a time it looked as though she might be used as a hotel at Bristol in England. Meanwhile, the *Vancouver Island Princess*, idle for two and a half years at Esquimalt, was sold in July 1993 by Stena Rederi A B for operation in China.[58] With the departure of the *Vancouver Island Princess*, the last of the CPR's passenger carrying *Princesses* had left the Pacific Coast forever. With the scrapping of the *Princess Marguerite* and the sale of the *Princess of Vancouver* in the early 1990s, the coastal liner era of the *Princesses* came to a sad and irretrievable end. Not even the *Louise*, the *Elaine* or the *Norah* who found temporary reprieves, survive to grace the future with their stories of the past and the elegance of their times.

As a postscript to the story, the political pendulum swung again in 1991 and the British Columbia government under NDP Premier Mike Harcourt re-established ferry service between Victoria and Seattle in 1994 with the transfer of the *Queen of Burnaby* from B.C. Ferries. Renamed the *Royal Victorian*, the refitted and very pleasant vessel operated from Victoria to Seattle during the summers of 1994-96 under the auspices of the Royal Victoria Line. Then in a privatization move the operation was taken over by Clipper Navigation, which renamed the ferry the *Princess Marguerite III* and redecorated her with huge red, white and blue Union Jacks. But after three summers of operation Clipper cancelled the service and in 2000 the *Queen of Burnaby* returned to B.C. Ferries. Clipper, however, continues its successful fast passenger ferry services between Seattle and Victoria.

EPILOGUE: *Finished With Engines*

IT IS EASY TO BE CRITICAL OF DECISIONS when looking back with the wisdom of passing years; it is far harder to be clairvoyant and predict change a decade into the future. And if the CPR erred in remaining too conservative and in not making the great leaps of investment and imagination that would have been required in the late 1940s and 1950s to maintain its role on the coast, they did not give way without a noble effort and a feeling of obligation to the people of the coast. It is hard to give up half a century of tradition and pride in service for new ways that emphasized speed, terminal efficiency and a no-frills operation over service and elegance.

The last vestiges of the British Columbia Coast Steamship Service were the rail and truck ferries operating between Vancouver and Nanaimo. Canadian Pacific, whose barge operations were by then called CP Rail System Coastal Marine Operations, abandoned its Vancouver harbour transfer facilities in October 1995 when a new terminal was opened at Tilbury on the Fraser River. The CPR owned three vessels in this service: the *Trailer Princess*, sold in 1993, the *Carrier Princess* and the *Princess Superior*. On November 16, 1998, Canadian Pacific sold its remaining marine operations to Dennis Washington, a U.S. operator of tugs and railroads, and they have continued operating as Seaspan Coastal Intermodal.

All attempts to replace the *Princess Marguerite* with more modern vessels on the service between Victoria and Seattle met with failure. As ferry operations they were not competitive with the shorter and faster routes. Moreover, they were not and could not be the elegant *Princesses* of such fond recall. The *Queen of Prince Rupert* disguised as the *Victoria Princess* or the *Queen of Burnaby*, paraded as the *Royal Victorian* and later as the *Princess Marguerite III*, could only masquerade; as pleasant as the trips were, they were still just ferry rides, not a ride on a genuine steamship whose lineage was unmistakable and irresistible, but all too sadly, ultimately uneconomic.

The *Princesses* were indeed irreplaceable and it was the unfolding of newer times, different technologies and societal demands that passed them by. It was almost as if they knew that to accommodate the coming changes along the coast, they would have to change so much themselves that they would lose the essence of what had made them special and memorable. Instead, as if tired from the long years, one by one, quietly, they faded away.

But the question lingers: could not a little imagination, just a twinkle of vision beyond the obvious and the mundane, a hint of creativity in a sea of often uncaring and uninspired political and civic leadership, have saved at least the *Marguerite*, in some form for future generations? There were so many possibilities and the voices were there but too few were

Chief Engineer Bill Neilson O.B.E., on the *Princess Kathleen* in 1947, was one of countless Coast Service mariners whose professionalism was the essence and the heart of the *Princess* steamships. –EARL J. MARSH COLLECTION

Passages

Over nearly a century, the Canadian Pacific operated steamships and motor vessels along the rugged, beautiful and hazardous Pacific Coast. Thousands of skilled, professional mariners, like Chief Engineer Bill Neilson, served on the *Princesses* and took them through some of the most difficult coastal waters in the world. At the same time, passenger services established the standards of their times. Maintaining the consistency of service that was so well remembered on the Coast Service reflected well on the officials of the steamship line and the officers and crew members of every one of the *Princesses*.

The CPR was renowned for its fine food and service; excellent catering was a hallmark of the company. The majority of the cooks who prepared the hundreds of thousands of meals on the *Princesses* were of Chinese descent. For many men, working on the *Princesses* was a lifetime career. Lam Sar Ning, a senior cook, for example, served on the boats for 43 years and Chief Cook John Kung, a native of Victoria, proudly received a gold pass from the company for 50 years of exemplary service. Long ago, that quiet gentleman showed me his pass and we talked about his days on the ships. He recalled starting in 1925 as a mess boy on the new *Kathleen* and later as a junior cook beginning his day at 5:30 a.m., with almost no time off, and his years as chief cook on the *Motor Princess* and later on the *Kathleen* and *Marguerite* when 12- to 13-hour days were still common. And of how he organized a meeting with the other senior cooks and management to negotiate for better working conditions, overtime and shorter shifts.

So many people worked behind the scenes: in purchasing, stores, accounts, or handling baggage; in repairing, painting and maintaining the ships; in coaxing aging boilers and engines along from deep in the bowels of an old *Princess*, or, in the early days, shovelling endless tons of coal in the suffocating heat of the boiler rooms; preparing wonderful meals in the hot kitchens; changing endless linens and cleaning staterooms, or dumping chamber pots; caring for a lost child or a young traveller making a steamship voyage without a parent; chipping ice from the decks; loading cargo at remote ports in the worst of weather; navigating through fog and Pacific storms; and on and on. Endless hours of endless chores.

My sadness is that we cannot remember them all individually. Their achievement was remarkable and the personality and affection that we so often attach to the beautiful steamships is in many ways a reflection of the people who brought them to life.

The story behind the *Princesses* was, fundamentally, one of business and commerce; they were not operated out of sentiment or for reasons of aesthetics. When business moved to other transport modes, the fate of the *Princesses* was sealed. But it would take a hard heart indeed not to appreciate the other qualities of this service and the elegance and grace they brought to generations of travellers in British Columbia, Washington and Alaska.

    –ROBERT D. TURNER.

Who could have witnessed the *Princess Elizabeth* steaming away from Seattle through the quiet waters of Elliott Bay for the last time in 1959 and not shed a tear? Her deep, resonant whistle echoed from Queen Anne Hill and the city skyline before fading away over the darkening waters of Puget Sound and soon she was gone. –JOE D. WILLIAMSON, LORNE CAMPBELL COLLECTION

listening and not enough seemed to care or at least, no one had the combination of vision, capital, pragmatism and love of a heritage resource to realize an alternative future for this the last of the coastal liners. Continued operations of the *Marguerite* were probably impractical but as a shoreside heritage centre in some form there might have been a lasting and important role for her in either Victoria or Seattle.

Now only memories remain, and the smaller artifacts, photos and documents that will be the last tangible reminders of these once and wonderful *Princess* steamships. They left a legacy in the history of the Pacific Coast from Seattle to Skagway and in Victoria and Vancouver and a hundred anchorages and harbours, that will not soon fade away. Perhaps that is all anyone can ask.

But on winter nights when fog swirls around Trail Island and there is a stillness across the strait and down through Puget Sound, could that be the deep whistle of the *Princess Victoria*, or perhaps the *Marguerite*, somewhere in the grey darkness far out over the sea?

Advertising for the West Coast service featured themes of spectacular scenery and First Nations cultures including the opportunity for travellers to purchase basketry. The representation of totem poles was often more caricature than accurate depiction, reflecting the widely held misunderstanding of the symbolism, function and highly-developed stylistic forms employed by the Native artists. —Author's collection, at left; Dr. W. B. Chung collection

Alaska service passenger list from 1936 and a brochure from 1941 with very dramatic interpretations of the Inside Passage. —Dr. W. B. Chung collection, above; and Lester G. Arellanes collection

The *Princess* fleet has every berth in Victoria's Inner Harbour occupied in this photo from about 1928. From left the *Princesses* in the background are the *Marguerite* or *Kathleen*, the old *Charmer*, the *Charlotte* and *Louise*. In the foreground are the *Mary*, *Royal*, *Island Princess* and *Motor Princess*. –Dr. W. Kaye Lamb collection, Vancouver Maritime Museum

APPENDIX 1: *The Princess Fleet*

Vessel	Gross Tons	Pass. Cap.	Dimensions*	Builder, launch date and summary. Engines: Triple-expansion unless noted. Scr. indicates screw propulsion. Sc. indicates scrapped.
*Charmer***	1944	500	200x39x13	Union Iron Works, 1887, as *Premier*. Collided with *Willamette*, Bush Point, WA, Oct. 18, 1892. To Victoria, renamed *Charmer*; sold 1935 and sc. 1 scr.
Hating/Princess May	1394 / 1717	350 / 500	249x33x18	Hawthorn, Leslie & Co., 1888. Ex *Mei Shih, Cass, Arthur, Cass, Ningchow*; renamed *Princess May*, 1902; *rebuilt* 1906 with enlarged cabins; sold 1919 for fruit service, sunk 1930s. 2 scr.
Princess Victoria	1940 / 3167	1000	300x41x18 / 300x58x18	C.S. Swan & Hunter, Nov. 18, 1902. Engines: Hawthorn, Leslie & Co. *Rebuilt* 1929 to increase automobile capacity; last voyage, Aug. 21, 1950; sold 1952, used as barge *Tahsis*, sunk Mar. 1953 in Welcome Pass. 2 scr.
Princess Beatrice	1290	350	193x37x15	B.C. Marine Railways, Sept. 9, 1903, wooden hull. Retired and sold for scrap 1928. 1 scr.
Princess Royal	1997	800	228x40x17	B.C. Marine Railways, Sept. 1, 1906, wooden hull. Boilers & Engines: Bow McLachlan & Co. Sold to Harold Elworthy in 1933, sc. Victoria. 1 scr.
Princess Charlotte	3845	1200	330x47x24	Fairfield Co., June 27, 1910. Sold to Typaldas Bros., Greece, 1949 and rebuilt, renamed *Mediterranean*, sc.1965. 2 scr. Capacity as high as 1500.
Princess Adelaide	3060	1200	291x46x15	Fairfield Co., July 7, 1910. Modified for North Coast service, 1932, by Yarrows. Sold to Typaldas Bros., Greece, as *Angelika*, sold for sc. 1967. 1 scr.
Princess Mary	1697 / 2155	600	210x40x14 / 248x40x14	Bow, McLachlan & Co., Sept. 21, 1910. *Lengthened* 1914. Retired 1951, sold 1952 for barge. Section of superstructure to Island Tug & Barge as Princess Mary Restaurant, Victoria. Hull as barge *Bulk Carrier No. 2*. Sunk Apr. 15, 1954. 2 scr.
Princess Alice	3099	1200	291x46x14	Swan, Hunter & Wigham Richardson, May 29, 1911. Engine by Wallsend Slipway & Eng., Wallsend. Sold to Typaldas Bros., Greece, renamed *Aegaeon*, wrecked 1966. 1 scr.
Princess Sophia	2320	500	245x44x12	Bow, McLachlan & Co., Nov. 8, 1911. Sunk on Vanderbilt Reef, Oct. 25, 1918.
Princess Patricia (I)	1158	900-960	270x32x15	Wm. Denny & Bros., Aug. 4, 1902. as *Queen Alexandria*, damaged by fire, purchased by CPR 1911; rebuilt Denny & Bros., sc. Victoria, 1937. Turbines 3 scr. (originally 5 scr.).
Princess Maquinna	1777	300	233x38x17	B.C. Marine Railways, Dec. 24, 1912. Engine and boilers: Bow, McLachlan & Co. Sold 1953, used as barge *Taku*, sc. 1962. 1 scr.
Princess Margaret	5934	2000	395x54x20	Wm. Denny & Bros., June 24, 1914. Not used by BCCSS; chartered by British Admiralty, Dec. 26, 1914 - April 27, 1919, used as minelayer; sold to Admiralty, refit 1921-23, sc. 1929. Geared turbines, 2 scr.
Princess Irene	5934	2000	395x54x20	Wm. Denny & Bros., June 24, 1914. Not used by BCCSS; chartered by British Admiralty, Jan. 20, 1915, as minelayer; blew up at Sheerness, 1915. Geared turbines, 2 scr.
Island Princess	339	60	116x25x8	M. McDowell, 1913. Engine by S. F. Hodge. Purchased by BCCSS 1918. Sold 1929 to S. Mathson and in 1930 to Gulf Islands Ferry Company, rebuilt to auto ferry, renamed *Cy Peck*. To B.C. Ferries, 1961; sold 1966 to J. H. Todd & Sons; sold 1975 to W & S Logging; sold 1981 to D. K. Forsburg; scuttled 1986. 1 scr.
Princess Louise (II)	4032	1000	317x48x17	Wallace Shipbuilding & Dry Dock, Aug. 29, 1921. Laid up 1962, sold 1965 as restaurant, San Pedro, CA; closed 1989; sank at dry-dock, raised but sank 1990 under tow for scuttling. 1 scr.
Motor Princess	1243	400	170x43x12	Yarrows Ltd., Mar. 31, 1923. Wooden hull. Diesels by McIntosh & Seymour. Removed passenger service 1950, used for freight, retired Oct. 17, 1953. Sold to Gulf Islands Ferry Co. 1955, rebuilt; to B.C. Ferries, 1961, as *Pender Queen*; sold 1981. Became fishing camp *Pender Lady*. 2 scr.
Princess Kathleen	5875	1800	350x60x20	John Brown & Co., Sept. 27, 1924. Chartered 1941-46 as transport, Mediterranean; rebuilt for Alaska and Triangle Route, 1947. Sunk at Lena Point, Alaska, Sept. 7, 1952. Compound turbines, 2 scr.
Princess Marguerite (I)	5875	1800	350x60x20	John Brown & Co., Nov. 29, 1924. Chartered 1941-42 as transport, Mediterranean. Torpedoed and sunk in Mediterranean 1942. Compound turbines, 2 scr.
Princess Elaine	1140	1200	291x48x16	John Brown & Co., Oct. 26, 1927. Sold 1963 as a restaurant vessel near Seattle, dismantled, 1976. Geared turbines, 3 screws.
Princess Norah	2731	450	250x48x17	Fairfield Co., Sept. 27, 1928. Bow rudder. Jointly operated with CNR as *Queen of the North*, 1955-57, sold 1958 to Northland Navigation as *Canadian Prince*, sold 1964 as *Beachcomber* restaurant at Kodiak, and eventually dismantled. 1 scr.
Princess Elizabeth	5251	1100	351x52x19	Fairfield Co., Jan. 16, 1930. Sold to Epirotiki Line, Greece, as *Pegasus*; to L. Dupes & Assoc. as *Highland Queen*, 1971; sc. 1976 Quadruple-expansion, 2 scr.
Princess Joan	5251	1100	351x52x19	Fairfield Co., Feb. 4, 1930. Sold to Epirotiki Line, Greece, as *Hermes*; to L. Dupes & Assoc., sc. 1974. Quadruple-expansion, 2 scr.
Princess Marguerite (II)	5911	2000	355x56x20	Fairfield Co., May 26, 1948. Car space increased 1973. Sold to B.C. Steamship Co. (1975) Ltd., 1975; Stena Line 1989; to Sea Containers 1991; sc. 1996 Alang, India. Turbo-electric, 2 scr.
Princess Patricia (II)	5911 / 6062	2000 / 1000	355x56x20	Fairfield Co., Oct. 6, 1948. *Rebuilt* for Alaska service 1963. Retired 1981; sold to Hempstead Holdings as hotel at Expo 86, Vancouver. Sold by court order to recover assets of Great American Cruise Lines, 1988 to Chi Shun Hua Steel Co., sc. Kaohsiung, Taiwan 1989. Turbo-electric, 2 scr.
Princess of Nanaimo	6787	1500-1750	344x62x20	Fairfield Co., Sept. 14, 1950. To east coast, 1963, as *Princess of Acadia*; withdrawn 1971; renamed *Henry Osborne*, as car transport; sc. 1974. Geared turbines, 2 scr.
Princess of Vancouver	5554	800-1200	388x63x20	A. Stephens & Co., Mar. 7, 1955. Re-engined 1973, car space increased. Sold 1981 to B.C. Ministry of Highways; to B.C. Steamship Co. (1975) Ltd. as *Vancouver Island Princess* in 1987; 1989 to Stena Line; retired Nov. 16, 1990. Sold 1993 to Stephanie Shipping, China, renamed *Nan Hai Ming Zhu*. 2 scr.

The fleet included the freighters *Princess Ena* (1908-34), *Nootka* (1926-55), *Princess of Alberni* (1953-58) and *Yukon Princess* (1951-58). The BCCSS added the coastal steamers *City of Nanaimo* and *Joan* and the tug *Czar* when the CPR acquired the Esquimalt & Nanaimo Railway in 1905. CPR also operated the rail and truck ferries *Trailer Princess* (1966), *Carrier Princess* (1973) and *Princess Superior* built in 1973, and acquired for service in B.C. in 1993. BCCSS tugs: *Dola, Qualicum, Nanoose, Nitinat* and *Kyuquot*. The *Point Grey, Prospect Point* and others were chartered.

*Registered length, breadth and depth in feet. The overall length of vessels was usually greater. Rebuilt dimensions are in italics.

**Earlier vessels from the Canadian Pacific Navigation Co. in 1901 are listed on page 12. Note: passenger capacity figures are representative licensed numbers and varied over the years with service needs.

The *Princess Maquinna* was the mainstay of the West Coast of Vancouver Island Service for nearly 40 years. She was photographed arriving at Victoria on December 26, 1948, by Maurice Chandler. –Author's Collection

APPENDIX 2: *Princess Genealogy*

1) PASSENGER VESSELS

Princess Louise (I), named for the daughter of Queen Victoria, the wife of the Marquis of Lorne. He was Governor General of Canada in 1878 when the vessel was acquired by the Hudson's Bay Company.

Princess May, named for the Duchess of York, later Queen Mary, the wife of George V. The Duke and Duchess of Cornwall and York toured Canada in 1901, the year the *Princess May* was acquired.

Princess Victoria, named for Princess Victoria, daughter of King Edward VII and a grand-daughter of Queen Victoria. The recent death of Queen Victoria and the fact that Victoria was the headquarters of the new steamship service also made the name very appropriate.

Princess Beatrice, named for the youngest daughter of Queen Victoria.

Princess Royal, named to honour Princess Louise, Duchess of Fife, the daughter of Edward VII. The title was bestowed on her in 1905.

Princess Charlotte, named for a grand-daughter of Queen Victoria and the daughter of Emperor Frederick of Germany.

Princess Adelaide, named for the mother of Queen Mary, the wife of King George V and the Duchess of Teck who had been Princess Mary Adelaide of Cambridge.

Princess Alice, named for the daughter of Queen Victoria's son, the Duke of Albany.

Princess Patricia (I), named for the younger daughter of the Duke of Connaught, who was a son of Queen Victoria and who became Governor General of Canada in 1912. With her parents, Princess Patricia toured western Canada in 1912, the year the steamer entered service.

Princess Mary, named for the daughter of King George V and Queen Mary. She too was named the Princess Royal.

Princess Sophia, named for Princess Sophie, a grand-daughter of Queen Victoria and daughter of Emperor Frederick of Germany.

Princess Maquinna, named for the daughter of Chief Maquinna, the Nuu-Chah-Nulth leader who met Capt. Cook and Capt. Vancouver in the late 1700s at Nootka Sound. CPR officials did not understand Nuu-Chah-Nulth naming traditions.

Princess Margaret, named for the elder daughter of the Duke of Connaught.

Princess Irene, named for a grand-daughter of Queen Victoria. Princess Irene of Hesse was married to Prince Henry of Prussia, a younger brother of Kaiser Wilhelm. The *Princess Irene* originally was to have been named *Princess Melita* after the daughter of the Duke of Edinburgh but the name was changed because there was another vessel with that name. However, in 1918 the CPR cabin-class liner *Melita*, although not a *Princess*, was completed and placed in North Atlantic service.

Island Princess, named for the Gulf Islands service for which the vessel was acquired.

Princess Louise (II), named for the first *Princess Louise* and indirectly for Queen Victoria's daughter.

Motor Princess, named because of its role as an automobile ferry and because of its diesel propulsion.

Princess Marguerite (I), named for the Hon. Marguerite Shaughnessy, daughter of the former CPR president, Lord Shaughnessy (formerly Sir Thomas Shaughnessy).

Princess Kathleen, named by CPR President Sir Edward Beatty, Shaughnessy's successor as president in 1918, for his life-long friend Miss Kathleen Madill. One of Thomas Shaughnessy's daughters was Marguerite Kathleen Shaughnessy and her name also may well have influenced the choice of name for the steamer.

Princess Elaine, origin uncertain.

Princess Norah, origin uncertain.

Princess Joan, named for the old steamer *Joan*, which was named for Joan Dunsmuir, wife of Robert Dunsmuir, coal baron and principal in the Esquimalt & Nanaimo Railway on Vancouver Island.

Princess Elizabeth, named for Princess Elizabeth, who later became Queen Elizabeth II, elder daughter of King George VI and Queen Elizabeth.

Princess Marguerite (II), named to commemorate the first *Princess Marguerite*, sunk during the Second World War.

Princess Patricia (II), named to commemorate the vessel scrapped in the 1930s.

Princess of Nanaimo, named for the city the steamer was intended to serve.

Princess of Vancouver, named in complementary fashion for the other major city on the Vancouver–to–Nanaimo service for which the vessel was built.

2) FREIGHTERS AND TRUCK FERRIES

Princess Ena (freighter), named for Princess Victoria Eugenie Julia Ena of Battenberg, daughter of Princess Beatrice, and a grand-daughter of Queen Victoria. In 1906 she married Alfonso XIII, King of Spain.

Princess of Alberni, named for the city of Alberni, one of the largest communities on the West Coast of Vancouver Island.

Yukon Princess, named for the Yukon territory, the vessel being acquired for the Skagway service.

Trailer Princess, named for its function, primarily as a ferry for semi-trailer trucks.

Carrier Princess, named for its primary function as a rail and truck ferry.

Princess Superior, renamed from the *Incan Superior*, a vessel used on the St. Lawrence River 1974-1993, to become the last addition to the CPR's *Princess* fleet before the sale of the remaining vessels.

END NOTES

[1] Quoted by Capt. James Anderson in *The Morning Star*, March 4, 1926.

[2] *Annual Report*, Canadian Pacific Railway, 1901.

[3] *Circular No. 1*, British Columbia Coast Service, May 23, 1903, issued by James W. Troup.

[4] Troup's title was later changed to Manager.

[5] *Daily Times*, Victoria, Oct. 12, 1901, p. 9 and Canadian Pacific Railway, *Timetable*, Nov. 29, 1901. p. 41.

[6] Builder's specifications, courtesy Earl Marsh. The reference to a Swedish vessel as the source of the design for the engines is from Hacking and Lamb, p. 195, and would explain the often-repeated stories that she had a warship's engines. Crew members resented any suggestion that the *Vic* had second-hand engines which she certainly did not, and this explanation is most logical.

[7] From Seattle *Post-Intelligencer* (?), April 2, 1904; clipping Earl Marsh collection.

[8] Alex W. Dow to Earl Marsh, Feb. 7, 1965, and Feb. 27, 1965. He retired from the Coast Service as Chief Engineer on the *Princess Victoria* on January 31, 1946.

[9] Troup to Arthur Piers, Dec. 22, 1902.

[10] This series of photos probably represents the work of two photographers. Some apparently earlier views show no photographer's credit while others, apparently from the 1920s, are credited to a photographer named Brigden. Interestingly, some of these photos are identified as being of the *Princess Louise* or *Princess Charlotte*, of which interior views, using same models, were taken. However, these photos are much more likely of the *Princess Victoria* based on the type of construction and the details of the cabins evident in accommodation plans and written descriptions. Troup's first major propeller-driven steamship, the *Victorian*, with many similarities to the *Princess Victoria*, is described by Clinton Betz in "The Victorian of 1891" in *The Sea Chest*, Vol. 23, No. 2, Dec. 1989, pp. 52-63.

[11] Often spelled Brochie Ledge.

[12] Financial statement and route map, 1912, Earl Marsh collection.

[13] *Daily Colonist*, June 6, 1913 and *Canadian Railway & Marine World*, (hereafter *CR&MW*), July 1911, p. 689 and Nov. 1911, p. 1075. Also builders specifications

and correspondence, Earl Marsh collection.

[14] *CR&MW*, Aug. 1913, p. 401, Aug. 1914, p. 391 and Jan. 1915, p. 36.

[15] Dr. W. B. Chung collection.

[16] Descriptions of the *Victoria's* trials and delivery voyage, *Daily Colonist*, Victoria, Mar. 29, 1903, p. 1.

[17] "May be World's Steaming Record," *Daily Colonist*, Victoria, May 1911. Clipping, Earl Marsh collection.

[18] Detailed memo, ca. 1912, Earl Marsh Collection. See also *CR&MW* April 1913, p. 95. The later report gave somewhat higher savings.

[19] See Ken Coates and Bill Morrison's *The Sinking of the Princess Sophia, Taking the North Down With Her* (1990). This book places the disaster in the context of the social and economic impact on the Yukon and Alaska from where most of the passengers were travelling. They also examine in detail the questions of whether or not the passengers might have been taken off before the ship sank. Pages 176-186 provide a passenger list and discussion of the number of people on board. See also: *The Final Voyage of the Princess Sophia: Did They Have to Die?* by Betty O'Keefe and Ian Macdonald (1998) for another extensive account of the tragedy, and Clinton Betz's excellent two-part article "The Princess Sophia" in *The Sea Chest*, Vol. 25 Nos. 1&2, Sept. and Dec. 1991. pp. 21-30 and 82-89.

[20] As recalled by Vancouver Island historian George Nicholson in the *Daily Colonist*, Oct. 21, 1951. See also *Vancouver Province*, Dec. 23, 1936.

[21] Troup to D. C. Coleman, Oct. 31, 1922.

[22] F. M. Rattenbury to Troup, July 9, 1923.

[23] *CR&MW*, Dec. 1924, p. 602.

[24] Details of Pier A from Vancouver City Archives, Ad Mss. 42, File 4, courtesy Leonard McCann. See also *CR&MW*, Mar. 1917, p. 107 and Mar. 1918, pp. 89-92.

[25] *CR&MW*, May 1924, p. 224 and Sept. 1926, p. 462, Oct. 1926, pp. 513-515, and Aug. 1927, p. 458.

[26] Clipping, *Daily Colonist*, November 1923.

[27] Reports of seating capacity vary from about 159 or 160 to 173. Seating was apparently expanded after the vessels were introduced to the Triangle Service.

[28] Troup to Harlan Smith, March 22, 1924.

[29] *Port of Seattle Bulletin*, Sept.- Oct. 1930.

[30] Troup to D.C. Coleman, Dec. 16, 1925.

[31] Letter to the author, February 8, 1974.

[32] See *Daily Colonist*, Victoria, Dec. 14 and 15, 1928.

[33] *CR&MW*, Oct. 1928, p. 628.

[34] Troup to C. E. Stockdill, Assistant to Vice-President, Winnipeg, Oct. 31, 1927.

[35] Dr. C. S. Douglas, consulting naval architect, to Capt. Cyril Neroutsos, Nov. 16, 1928. SS *Princess Norah, Report on Trials.*

[36] George Nicholson, "SS *Princess Maquinna*: Friend of the Up-Islanders," *Daily Colonist* (Magazine Section) Oct. 21, 1951, p. 7.

[37] These incidents are recorded in the Earl Marsh Collection including official incident reports and documents, correspondence and clippings. Other sources include: *The Daily Colonist*, Victoria, Feb. 6, 1919 with further details from Ken Gibson, Tofino; the case of the *Maquinna's* collision with the *Masunda* was heard before Mr. Justice Bateson, High Court of Justice, Admiralty Division, October 10, 1934; and *The Daily Colonist*, Victoria, "Worst Run in the World" by Archie Wills, Dec. 19, 1976, pp. 4-5. The *Carelmapu* loss was described by Capt. Gillam in Victoria's *Daily Times*, Nov. 25, 1915, and reports in the *Colonist* Nov. 26 and 27, 1915, courtesy Neil Robertson.

[38] Troup to C.E. Stockdill, Winnipeg, November 14, 1927; Neroutsos to DesBrisay, Vancouver, June 5, 1929.

[39] Lloyd M. Stadum, "The Race I Remember," *The Sea Chest*, vol.4. no. 3, Mar. 1971, pp. 111-113.

[40] Capt. Neroutsos to J. H. Alexander, Superintendent Engineer, April 5, 1930.

[41] B. Robinson of Yarrows Ltd. to Capt. Neroutsos, Dec. 23, 1931, and *Specifications for Proposed Alterations to S.S. Princess Adelaide.* August 27, 1931.

[42] From BCCSS, *Statement Showing Number of days Steamers Laid up and in Commission during 1932.* March 10, 1933. Earl Marsh Collection.

[43] Memorandum to C. E. Stockdill, re SS *Princess Royal*, Feb. 1933.

[44] *CR&MW*, May 1931, p. 280 and Merilees, 1998, *Newcastle Island, A Place of Discovery.*

[45] From *British Columbia Coast Steamship Service*, an address by C. E. Stockdill before the Montreal Adult Education Group, Feb. 20, 1940.

[46] Based on deck plans of the *Princess Kathleen* during war service, 1941-1945, Earl Marsh Collection.

[47] Quoted by George Musk in "The Princesses-from the Triangle Services to troop carrying," *Seanews*, March, 1975. This article also provided additional details about the ships' movements during the war.

[48] A copy of Capt. Leicester's "Secret" report is in the Earl Marsh collection as is a memo quoting Engineer Harris.

[49] *Daily Times*, Victoria, Aug. 2, 1946. Earlier details from *Princess Kathleen* voyage reports.

[50] *Daily Times*, Victoria, Jan. 11 and 16, 1955; June 27, 1956.

[51] See *Daily Colonist*, Oct. 26, 1974.

[52] *Daily Colonist*, April 1, 1975 and *Post-Intelligencer*, Seattle, Apr. 2, 1974.

[53] *Daily Colonist*, Apr. 23, 1975 and *The Victorian*, Apr. 23, 1975 and Apr. 28, 1975.

[54] *Daily Colonist*, May 1, 1975. See for example Gorde Hunter's column. See also George Oake's column "On the Good Ship Politics," *Daily Colonist*, June 3, 1975.

[55] Apparently the B.C. Government wrote down its assets in the B.C. Steamship Company by $11 million before the sale. See *Times-Colonist*, Nov. 16, 1990.

[56] A Stena circular to employees gave a substantially higher figure.

[57] *Daily Colonist*, Nov. 15 & 16, 1990.

[58] *Times-Colonist*, July 23, 1993.

Since this project began several key collections are now in the exemplary care of major institutions. Earl Marsh, who passed away in 1999, left his extensive collection of Coast Service material to the British Columbia Archives in Victoria and Dr. Wally Chung donated his wonderful CPR collection to Special Collections of the University of British Columbia Library. The late Joe D. Williamson's outstanding marine photos are now at the Puget Sound Maritime Historical Society in Seattle.

REFERENCES

Coates, Ken and Bill Morrison. 1990. *The Sinking of the Princess Sophia, Taking the North Down with Her.* Oxford University Press, Toronto, ON.

Greene, Ruth. 1969. *Personality Ships of British Columbia.* Marine Tapestry Publications Ltd., West Vancouver, B.C.

Hacking, Norman and W. Kaye Lamb. 1974. *The Princess Story, A Century of West Coast Shipping.* Mitchell Press, Vancouver, B.C.

Henry, Tom. 1998. *Westcoasters. Boats that Built B.C.* Harbour Publishing Co., Madeira Park, B.C.

Hilton, George. 1968. *The Night Boat.* Howell-North Books, Berkeley, CA.

Lamb, W. Kaye. 1977. *History of the Canadian Pacific Railway.* Macmillan Publishing, New York.

Lamb, W. Kaye. 1991. *Empress to the Orient.* Vancouver Maritime Museum, Vancouver, B.C.

Merilees, Bill. 1998. *Newcastle Island, A Place of Discovery.* Heritage House, Surrey, B.C.

Musk, George. 1981. *Canadian Pacific, The Story of the Famous Shipping Line.* Holt Rinehart and Winston of Canada, Toronto, ON.

Newell, Gordon (Ed.). 1966. *The H. W. McCurdy Marine History of the Pacific Northwest.* Superior Publishing Company, Seattle, WA.

Newell, Gordon and Joe Williamson. 1959. *Pacific Coastal Liners.* Superior Publishing Co., Seattle, WA.

Nicholson, George. 1962. *Vancouver Island's West Coast.* Published by the author, Victoria, B.C.

O'Keefe, Betty and Ian Macdonald. 1998. *The Final Voyage of the Princess Sophia: Did They All Have to Die?* Heritage House, Surrey, B.C.

Turner, Robert D. 1973 & 1998. *Vancouver Island Railroads.* Sono Nis Press, Victoria, B.C.

Turner, Robert D. 1977. *The Pacific Princesses, An Illustrated History of the Canadian Pacific's Princess Fleet on the Northwest Coast.* Sono Nis Press, Victoria, B.C.

Turner, Robert D. 1981. *The Princess Marguerite, Last of the Coastal Liners.* Sono Nis Press, Victoria, B.C.

Turner, Robert D. 1981. *The Pacific Empresses, An Illustrated History of the Canadian Pacific's Empress Liners on the Pacific Ocean.* Sono Nis Press, Victoria, B.C.

Turner, Robert D. 1984 & 1998. *Sternwheelers & Steam Tugs, An Illustrated History of the Canadian Pacific's British Columbia Lake & River Service.* Sono Nis Press, Victoria, B.C.

Wright, E. W. 1961. *Lewis and Dryden's Marine History of the Pacific Northwest.* Antiquarian Press, Ltd., New York, NY

General articles include:

Drake, Shawn J. 1997. "The *Princess* Line: British Columbia Coast Steamship Service," *Steamboat Bill.* Vol. 54, No. 3, pp.200-220.

Leithead, Robert C. 1967-68. "The Canadian Pacific Tri-City Route," *The Sea Chest*, Vol.1, Nos. 1-3.

CANADIAN PACIFIC RAILWAY COMPANY

BRITISH COLUMBIA
COAST STEAMSHIP SERVICE

Reminiscent of the night boats that had sailed on the Triangle Route for so many years, the *Princess Marguerite*, at left, was photographed at Seattle after arriving from Victoria in June 1981. The *Princess Patricia*, shown above steaming away from Vancouver on her route to Skagway, continued on the Alaska service until she was retired by Canadian Pacific in 1981. –ROBERT D. TURNER

INDEX